MICHIGAN STATE UNIVERSITY LIBRARY

Aug 2 2 2025

WITHDRAWN

PLACE IN RETURN BOX to remove this checkout from your record.
TO AVOID FINES return on or before date due.

DATE DUE	DATE DUE	DATE DUE
SCIENCE		

MSU Is An Affirmative Action/Equal Opportunity Institution

c:\circ\datedue.pm3-p.1

INSECT SCIENCE EDUCATION IN AFRICA: THE ICIPE GRADUATE SCHOOL MODEL

Proceedings

International Conference on Innovative Approaches for Sustainable Capacity Building for Insect Science Leadership in Africa

Bellagio, Italy
24–28 June, 1991

The Rockefeller Foundation

The International Centre of Insect Physiology and Ecology

QL
461
.I665
1991
c.2

CONTENTS

Introduction: Why 'Bellagio II'? ....(i)

Highlights of Discussions 1

Communique and Signatories 7

Welcome Remarks *T.R. Odhiambo* 13

Keynote Address *L.K.H. Goma* 19

Role of UNESCO in African Science *A. Badran* 23

Innovative Approaches for Sustainable Building for Insect Science
Leadership in Africa *M.T. Mapuranga* 37

Higher Education in Africa in the Last Three Decades: A Demographic
Overview *S.H. Ominde* 41

Postgraduate Programmes in Africa: Need for Innovative Approaches *J.S. Djangmah* ..55

Instituto Venezolano de Investigaciones Cientificas (IVIC) *H. Vanegas* 63

Role of Research Centres in Postgraduate Training in India *Y.P. Singh* 79

Multi-disciplinary Institutional Models for Graduate Training in
Insect Science *O.A. Adeyeye* 85

Innovative Linkages of Universities and Research Institutes:
ICIPE's Experience *Z.T. Dabrowski* 95

The Proposed ICIPE Graduate School: Concept and Rationale *T.R. Odhiambo* 111

List of Participants 121

Group Photo 125

WHY "BELLAGIO II" ?

In 1978, a committee of African leaders of academia, research and science policy development recommended that the Kenya-based International Centre of Insect Physiology and Ecology (ICIPE), in collaboration with African universities, initiate and develop an international postgraduate course leading to the M.Sc. and Ph.D. degrees in insect science.

The ensuing international dialogue culminated in the convening of the first International Conference on Postgraduate Education in Insect Science, held at the Rockefeller Foundation Bellagio Study and Conference Centre, Italy, in 1981. This first planning conference was attended by representatives of African universities, research institutions based in Africa, and by other participants from similar communities worldwide. The product of this **"Bellagio I Conference"** was the establishment of the African Regional Postgraduate Programme in Insect Science (ARPPIS), described in these Proceedings. This programme, managed by ICIPE, has achieved thus far a cumulative enrollment of 102 students, of whom about 50 have received their Ph.D.'s.

A **Task Force** appointed to review the structure and objectives of the ARPPIS programme recommended in its Final Report in 1989, the strengthening of the ARPPIS network by the establishment of an autonomous graduate school with the capacity to award its own degrees, and concentrating on the Ph.D. programme.

Ten years after Bellagio I, in June of 1991, the present conference, **"Bellagio II"**, was convened to specifically deliberate that recommendation of the Task Force: the establishment of a multi-disciplinary **ICIPE Graduate School** for the insect-related sciences, including entomology, ecology, sensory physiology, molecular biology, biochemistry, and so on. Present to discuss this proposition were an august assembly of Vice-Chancellors of African universities now participating in ARPPIS, as well as key representatives from prestigious research institutes based in the tropics, donor agencies and international scientific organisations.

The papers and discussions presented in these Proceedings describe the social, economic and academic climate prevailing in Africa, which together provide the rationale for the ICIPE Graduate School. Professor S. Ominde gives a demographic overview of the population pressures on institutions of higher education on the Continent, while Professors M.T. Mapuranga (OAU) and J.S. Djangmah (AAU) describe the crisis in science and technology training and the need for capacity building from their perspectives as elder statesmen-scientists. Dr. O.A. Adeyeye (ESA) stresses the need for a concerted, aggressive multi-disciplinary approach to insect science education. The acclaimed success of other postgraduate degree programmes offered by research centres located in the tropics is described in the papers by Prof. Y.P. Singh (IARI, India) and Dr. H. Vanegas (IVIC, Venezuela). UNESCO's role in supporting education and programmes in the natural sciences is described in the paper by Dr. A. Badran. And finally, the experiences and achievements of the ICIPE and of the ARPPIS programme are highlighted herein by Professors T.R. Odhiambo and Z.T. Dabrowski, respectively.

Together with a large number of African universities, an ICIPE Graduate School can help to develop the critical mass of insect scientists and pest management technologies needed to tackle many of Africa's most basic problems in agriculture and public health.

HIGHLIGHTS OF DISCUSSIONS

Introduction

In 1950, the average population growth rate in Africa was reported to be 2.1% per year; this rose to 3.0% per annum in 1980. The average growth rate in agricultural production was reported to be between 1.8%-2.0% per year for the period 1970-1985; however, an average growth rate of greater than 3.0% per annum is needed to cope with the rate of increasing population growth. These facts are stated to illustrate the desperate state of food production in Africa and to point out the amount of effort that is needed to correct the imbalance.

Increasing agricultural and livestock productivity is absolutely essential for the future well-being of African societies and can only be achieved through vigorous agricultural research. The research must be based on indigenous human resources capable of developing systems that are environmentally sustainable and economically viable for both the country and its farmers. History has shown that the science-oriented transformation of societies has required the development of indigenous human capital, dedicated to the long-term realisation of national development goals and motivated by incentives to reach the highest levels of excellence and relevance. Technical assistance by itself has failed, over the last quarter-century, to create the necessary conditions for sustainable agriculture in Africa.

The present African human capital in science and technology is relatively small. There are estimated to be some 20,000 research and development (R&D) specialists serving in about 250 R&D institutions in Africa south of the Sahara. If North Africa is included, there are only 32,000 R&D specialists in about 300 institutions servicing the entire continent. This leaves a huge science and technology gap – a dangerous human resource deficit which threatens any mission-oriented R&D programme for national development. Therefore, the rapid intensification of high-level training at the advanced degree and postdoctoral levels relying solely on the universities, is presently unrealistic.

Present State of African Universities

The Vice-Chancellors and representatives of the Association of African Universities (AAU) present at the Bellagio II Conference indicated that the current general economic crisis and the pressure for expansion of undergraduate education at the universities have adversely affected their postgraduate programmes. Recent review missions undertaken by the AAU confirm that universities are neither sufficiently well-equipped nor prepared to offer Ph.D. programmes. UNESCO's studies also confirm that Africa is under pressure from many crises and, therefore, it has neglected science education; what is needed is to identify centres of excellence to further its frontiers of science. UNESCO pledged its support for the most feasible and cost-effective models which will complement the universities in their development of human resources for the sciences.

Training African Scientific Leaders in Africa

The participants concurred that, whereas overseas training of African scholars costs between US$ 120,000 - 160,000 per student, the students often obtain irrelevant training. The projects for the Ph.D: theses are selected on the basis of the supervisors' scientific interests and departmental priorities, which are very often irrelevant to African needs. African problems are treated as "footnotes" to the research.

The difference between the facilities available in the developed countries and the students' home institutions causes a shock when the students return to their respective countries. The emphasis overseas is on the use of specialised high - technology equipment, and not on equipping African students with a range of techniques which they can later use after returning to their home countries. This difference in scientific approach is especially critical for the development of IPM technologies: for example, the developed countries emphasise profit-oriented farming but sustainability of yield is more important in Africa. Another disadvantage to overseas training was also recorded by the participants: a large number of African graduates have remained in the USA and Europe, increasing the 'brain-drain' from the continent.

It was noted that Africa has not yet utilised the scientific potential of centres of excellence for advanced training, in spite of recommendations made at meetings organised over the last five years by deans and directors of postgraduate studies, and the Association of Faculties of Agriculture in Africa (AFAA). These meetings have made strong recommendations to African countries to involve National Agricultural Research Systems (NARS), defined as "all institutions/organisations in a given country actually or potentially in agricultural research and technology development".

Models for Involving Research Centres in Advanced Education

Examples of successful models for involving centres of excellence in postgraduate training in India and Venezuela were described at the Conference. These centres offer much broader programmes than classical science departments at the universities. Newly-developed research centers in Africa have the potential to be involved in the postgraduate training to complement the national universities. These centres have the opportunity to offer inter-disciplinary programmes which the universities cannot offer.

Success of the African Regional Postgraduate Programme in Insect Science (ARPPIS)

The ICIPE, as a research centre, identified the need for advanced training in insect science in the 1970's, and following recommendations by the African Committee of the ICIPE Governing Council, established the African Regional Postgraduate Programme in Insect Science (ARPPIS). ARPPIS combines the excellence of the ICIPE with the academic experience of African universities developed from their successful Ph.D. programmes. ARPPIS presently involves 21 African universities participating with the ICIPE. Since 1986, 48 Ph.D. and M.Phil. students have graduated from the programme.[1]

However, the Task Force Review Committee, chaired by Prof. L.K.H. Goma, identified some deficiencies in the programme and concluded that the success of ARPPIS had been achieved with a structure that was inherently unstable. The Task Force made recommendations to establish four sub-regional centres for study leading to the MSc. in Insect Science. Further discussions concluded that ARPPIS should be strengthened by establishing these four centres and should also include the proposed ICIPE Graduate School.

---

[1] Detailed information regarding the administration, academic content, graduate training in insect science at the ICIPE, etc., is contained in a separate document entitled *Graduate Training in Insect Science at the ICIPE* (May 1991), by Thomas R. Odhiambo, Rhoda A. Odingo and Zbigniew T. Dabrowski.

The ICIPE Graduate School as a Model

The Vice-Chancellors present at this Conference were unanimous in supporting the establishment of the ICIPE Graduate School as a logical process in strengthening postgraduate training. They did not foresee any competition with the universities; rather, the programme will help prevent 'brain-drain' and promote 'brain circulation' within the continent. The Association of African Universities (AAU) confirmed this view.

The participants, therefore, agreed that the ICIPE, as a centre of excellence in insect science, should assist in establishing the ICIPE Graduate School, concentrating on the Ph.D. programme. The proposed Graduate School will consolidate the present ARPPIS Ph.D. programme and serve as a model for other research institutions in Africa. They emphasised that the ICIPE Graduate School programme should offer multi-disciplinary opportunities to students. The academic programme should offer state-of-the-art courses, not only in insect science, but also in such related disciplines as biostatistics and computer science, chemical ecology, molecular biology, genetics, research management and social science.

This model, in which an international research centre maintains strong links with universities, was encouraged by UNESCO. In effect, these 'supra-national' institutions will serve Africa well in identified disciplines in science.

Support and Funding for the Graduate School

Representatives to the 'Bellagio II Conference' from the Organisation of African Unity (OAU) supported the concept of establishing this new Ph.D. programme. UNESCO has already pledged its support for the proposed Graduate School by establishing a Professorial Chair for visiting professors, who will be invited for teaching and preparation of textbooks.

Representatives of the ICIPE Governing Council expressed their concern about the financial burden the Graduate School might impose on the Centre (ICIPE). However, the representatives of other research centres offering postgraduate training in India and South America, noted that the additional budget for postgraduate education comprised only a small portion of their centres' total budget, and that the scientific output of the research students far surpassed their training costs. They emphasised the valuable input the scholars made to achieving the centres' research objectives.

Representatives from Africa concurred that this new programme, based on the needs of the continent and contributing to the total development of Africa, be allowed to go forward. It was agreed that a consortium of agencies in international co-operation be encouraged to support and fund, in a co-ordinate way, facilities for this new model for graduate training in Africa.

COMMUNIQUE

We, representatives from universities, research institutions, the Organization of African Unity (OAU), Association of African Universities (AAU) and agencies of international cooperation, *realising* the urgent need for human resource development for capacity building in science in Africa; and *noting* that the present conditions in many African universities make it difficult to reach a critical mass that allows teaching and research supervision of postgraduate students, *accept* and *support* exploring innovative models in postgraduate education at Centres of Excellence.

Recognising the great importance of insects as vectors of human and livestock diseases and as pests of agricultural crops which limit productivity, *noting* the inadequate number of insect scientists in Africa and the need for collaboration in research and research training in order to use scarce resources to full advantage; *recognising* the mandate of the ICIPE to develop and promote insect science, especially methods of pest and vector management, essential for dealing with tropical environments; *appreciating* the significant impact on the training of African insect scientists, including an increasing number of women, achieved through the African Regional Postgraduate Programme in Insect Science (ARPPIS), a collaborative venture between the ICIPE and 21 African universities; and *noting* at the same time the numerous constraints, inherent in the systems of the individual universities,

We, therefore:

- *Agree* that training of African scientists abroad contributes to brain-drain and often takes place in an alien environment where African problems are considered 'footnotes' in the training programme.

- *Note* the urgent need for staff development, and *recognising* that the Ph.D. is a research degree requiring a critical mass of supporting and collaborating specialists, therefore, *recommend* pooling of resources at identified Centres of Excellence in Africa to complement the universities.

- *Agree* that the present ARPPIS Ph.D. Programme will be consolidated and enriched by the addition of a degree-awarding programme at the ICIPE within the ARPPIS network, *noting* that ARPPIS students will have the option of having the Ph.D. awarded by their registering University or by the ICIPE Graduate School.

- *Support* the consolidation and enhancement of the present ARPPIS Programme into an *academically autonomous* ICIPE Graduate School as a model for involving recognised Centres of Excellence concentrating on Ph.D. training.

- *Recommend* a broad multi-disciplinary approach in curriculum development and research projects of future Ph.D. theses which meet world standards. The programme will contain advanced courses and research work leading to a thesis, based on a flexible credit system with the possibility of transferring credits from other institutions. The quality of the programme will be enhanced through endowed Chairs for distinguished professors in disciplines that complement the expertise of the ICIPE staff.

- *Recommend* that the students be admitted through a competitive merit system.

- *Emphasise* that a major purpose of the ICIPE Graduate School will be to assist and benefit from universities in Africa through sabbatical, secondment and twinning arrangements, and through the development of teaching materials. African governments, non-governmental organisations, private enterprise and international bodies should be encouraged to actively support this scheme.

- *Recommend* that the ICIPE Graduate School interact, through the appropriate channels, with industry and private enterprise to draw on their cooperation in areas of mutual interest.

- *Recommend* that the ICIPE Graduate School becomes a partner in the expanded ARPPIS network embracing the M.Sc. degree-awarding Sub-Regional Centres and the ARPPIS participating universities. The network will further integrate, stimulate and enhance a partnership and regional cooperation.

- *Recommend* that a fee structure adequate to cover operating costs be instituted and that students seek fellowships from agencies to cover these; and that a *consortium* of agencies in international cooperation be encouraged to support, in a *coordinated way* (with the Sponsoring Group for the ICIPE), facilities for this new model for graduate training in Africa.

- *Recommend* that the Association of African Universities reviews the progress of this scheme after a suitable period to consider applying this model for other multi-disciplinary fields of demonstrated need.

In conclusion, we *recommend* that the Governing Council of the ICIPE embark on the establishment of the ICIPE Graduate School for the training of Ph.D. degree students in insect science as soon as the availability of resources makes it feasible.

Bellagio, Italy
27th June 1991

Signed	Institution
Professor Donald E. U. Ekong, Secretary-General	Association of African Universities, Ghana
Professor Chiweyite Ejike, Vice-Chancellor	Anambra State University of Technology, Nigeria
Professor Kunthala Jayaram, Director, Centre of Biotechnology	Anna University, India
Dr. Olusola A. Adeyeye, Representative for Africa, International Affairs Committee	Entomological Society of America (ESA), USA
Professor Y. P. Singh, Professor of Agricultural Extension	Indian Agricultural Research Institute (IARI), India
Dr. Horacio H. Vanegas, Director	Instituto Venezolano de Investigaciones Cientificas (IVIC), Venezuela
Professor Simeon Ominde, Professor of Geography	Institute of Population Studies (IPS), Kenya
Professor Thomas R. Odhiambo, Director, ICIPE	Chairman, ARPPIS Academic Board, Kenya
Professor George Eshiwani, Principal	Jomo Kenyatta University College of Agriculture and Technology (JKUCAT), Kenya
Professor Dr. Heinz Rembold, Head, Insect Biochemistry	Max Planck Institute for Biochemistry, Germany
Professor Lameck K. H. Goma, Minister	Ministry of Higher Education, Science and Technology, Zambia
Professor Maurice Ntahobari, Rector	National University of Rwanda, Rwanda

Professor James O. C. Ezeilo, Director	National Mathematical Centre, Nigeria
Dr. Oebele Bruinsma, Head, Africa Desk	Netherlands Organization for International Cooperation in Higher Education (NUFFIC), Netherlands
Dr. M. T. Mapuranga, Assistant Secretary-General	Organization of African Unity (OAU), Ethiopia
Professor Peter Esbjerg, Chairman Programme Committee	ICIPE Governing Council and Professor, Royal Veterinary and Agricultural University, Denmark
Dr. A. Badran, Assistant Director-General for Science	United Nations Educational, Scientific and Cultural Organization (UNESCO), France
Professor J. S. Djangmah, Head, Zoology Department	University of Ghana, Legon
Professor Muddathir D. Tingari, Vice-Chancellor	University of Khartoum, Sudan
Dr. Erik W. Thulstrup,* Education and Employment Division	The World Bank, USA
Professor Z. T. Dabrowski, Academic Coordinator	ARPPIS Missions on M.Sc. Sub-Regional Centres, Nairobi
Mrs. R. A. Odingo, Chief Planning Officer	International Centre of Insect Physiology and Ecology, Nairobi

*His views do not necessarily express official World Bank policy.

CONFERENCE PAPERS

WELCOME REMARKS

T. R. Odhiambo
*Director, The International Centre
of Insect Physiology and Ecology (ICIPE)
Nairobi, Kenya*

Early in the life of the International Centre of Insect Physiology and Ecology (the ICIPE), its Governing Board established two important policy advisory organs. The first, the so-called **International Committee**, was comprised of representatives of about 15 academies of science that have special interest in the advancement of insect science in the tropical world. The major concerns of the International Committee were the fostering and maintenance of excellence in research in this field, and the development of strong linkages with advanced research institutions around the world. The second policy advisory organ, the so-called **African Committee**, consisted of leading African personalities in academia, the research community, and the science policy community, including representatives of the key regional development agencies such as the United Nations Economic Commission for Africa (ECA). The African Committee's major concerns were the assurance of ICIPE's programme relevance to Africa's priority problems in pest and vector management, and the development of long-term linkages with the African scientific research and technological development (R&D) systems, at both national and regional levels.

Since ICIPE's origins are intimately related to the origins of the global sensitivity to the unsustainable environmental practices of the 1960s and before, and since it had become apparent that the pest control approaches of the immediate past had failed in the long-term, the world became aware that the new future-oriented technologies for industry and natural resource-based development were knowledge-intensive. R&D has become a major instrument for creating and acquiring this knowledge, while a keen sense of entrepreneurship has provided the mechanism for translating such knowledge into useful products and services. The minuscule and fragile R&D community in key segments of development-oriented science and technology (S&T) in Africa has characterised the continent since the 1960s. In the segment embracing tropical insect science and pest management, especially that associated with the emerging technologies for integrated pest management (IPM), Africa had negligible capacity in R&D, and certainly in high-level education and training, both in relation to human resources and R&D institutions.

Twelve and a half years ago, at its 9th Meeting held in December 1978, the African Committee reached a profound, historic recommendation. The policy recommendation was that the ICIPE, in collaboration with African universities, establish an international postgraduate course in insect science in Africa leading to the M.Sc. and Ph.D. degrees, with the ICIPE as the course manager. The context under which this policy statement was made was that "the facilities available at the ICIPE were unique and would make it possible to establish a high standard of international postgraduate course in insect science under African conditions". The strongly worded proposal that an advanced centre of scientific research (the ICIPE) should be put in charge of initiating and developing a university-type postgraduate degree programme in its area of competence, was a revolutionary, strategic idea of great interest to several personalities and institutions in Africa and elsewhere in the world. Perhaps this strategic decision stands out as the single most innovative idea in university postgraduate education in Africa during the 1970s.

The idea took a great deal of debating and deliberation for the next three years, while detailed planning went on alongside. This international dialogue culminated in the convening of the International Conference on Postgraduate Education in Insect Science at the Rockefeller Foundation Bellagio Study and Conference Center at Villa Serbelloni, Italy, in September 1981. The Conference was attended by 22 participants from Africa, Australia, Europe and North America, representing academia, the research community, and donor agencies. Nine African universities were represented, as well as three research institutions based in Africa. This Planning Conference (so-called Bellagio I) unanimously put forward a proposal to establish what soon became known as the **African Regional Postgraduate Programme in Insect Science (ARPPIS).** In April 1983, ARPPIS enrolled its first class of eight postgraduate scholars, all registering for the Ph.D. degree in insect science, with seven universities in Africa intimately taking part as Participating Universities in the work of the Academic Board.

In the eight years since ARPPIS became functional, there is no doubt that this specialised postgraduate education programme has become a resounding success. The number of first-rate candidates for selection has increased greatly, allowing the Academic Board to offer one place for every 5 or 6 very good candidates. The accumulative number of students enrolled in ARPPIS has now reached 102, with about 50 having passed their Ph.D. degrees; further, all successful graduates are still working in their professional fields within Africa. The African Participating Universities have climbed from the original seven to 21 now, with three more waiting to be admitted into this singular network. They represent all the sub-regions of Africa, including North Africa, and cover all the major language groups in the continent. The credibility of the ICIPE, as manager of this postgraduate education programme, is symbolised by the fact that ICIPE is represented, as an Observer, in the Southern African Conference of Vice-Chancellors, and ICIPE's candidature is currently being considered as an Associate Member of the Association of African Universities (AAU).

Even within this environment of success, it soon became apparent, within four years of the establishment of ARPPIS, that it was facing some serious problems that needed to be addressed. Some problems were concerned with operational difficulties: differing registration requirements by each of the Participating Universities; residential qualifications; the interval between submission of a thesis and the eventual examination of the candidate; the issue of cost-sharing between the ICIPE and the Participating Universities, etc. There were also questions of further development stemming from the original success itself, such as the increasing demand for M.Sc.-level training; the need for widening the range of subject matter in the dissertation phase; meeting the needs of French-speaking countries in Africa; and whether the education programme was leading to a significant diversion of ICIPE's resources – intellectual as well as financial – in relation to its primary mandate on R&D.

In order to more systematically address all these issues, the ICIPE commissioned a **Task Force** in May 1987 "to review the structure and objectives of existing graduate training at the ICIPE; to review the graduate training programme in similar institutions; to make recommendations for the future development of graduate training at the ICIPE, taking into account... the need to develop graduate training at the ICIPE sensitive to, and in the context of higher education in Africa; [and] to assess the implications of the recommendations for manpower requirements, physical facilities and funding".

The Task Force made its Final Report in May 1989, while its Chairman had held several periodic meetings in the interim with ICIPE's Governing Council and the ARPPIS Academic Board.

Among the major recommendations made by the Task Force in May 1989, three stand out as pertinent to this week's International Conference at Bellagio (Bellagio II):

- That there be established four **Sub-Regional Centres for the M.Sc. Degree in Insect Science**. The Host University in each Sub-Regional Centre would award its own degree, but would receive students for this course and thesis work from the Sub-Region's Collaborating Universities.

- That the ICIPE establish a **Graduate School**, with a focus on the Ph.D. degree in insect science. The ICIPE Graduate School would have the capacity to award its own degree.

- That the four Sub-Regional Centres and the ICIPE Graduate School would continue to be part of a strengthened ARPPIS network.

The publication of The Task Force Final Report has been followed by an intensive series of discussions within the ICIPE Governing Council and its organs, and by the ARPPIS Academic Board. The proposal on Sub-Regional Centres has been accepted, and selection missions have been mounted for all four sub-regions. As a result, three Sub-Regional Centres have been finally selected, and planning is going apace for their functionally coming into being between 1992 and 1994. The selection of the fourth Sub-Regional Centre is due to be completed this year. Further, the Vice-Chancellors of the four host universities are due to meet at the Jomo Kenyatta University College of Agriculture and Technology in Nairobi in August, 1991 together with the Vice-Chancellors of their Collaborating Universities. The main objective of the Vice-Chancellors' Meeting is to agree finally on curricula content and examinations, operational matters, funding, and management and coordination issues for the M.Sc. programme.

Bellagio II has been convened to specifically deliberate on the proposed ICIPE Graduate School, having behind it four years of continuing discussion and planning. The Graduate School idea is an exciting one for Africa, which is experiencing an acute long-running crisis in its higher education sector, more deeply so at the postgraduate level. The Graduate School idea is invaluable in at least three respects:

- *First*, basing the Graduate School in an advanced R&D institution both enriches while at the same time complements the universities' own programme of postgraduate education and research, because of ICIPE's comparative strength in its own relevant specialised area of R&D competence.

- *Second*, the antecedent Ph.D. programme at the ICIPE has established an excellent cooperative functional environment with a large number of African universities. These partners, together with the new Graduate School, may well be able to develop within Africa a critical mass of insect scientists and pest management technologists within the next two decades, if the proposals on the Ph.D. and M.Sc. programmes in the context of the ARPPIS network are empowered to go ahead as vigorously as the original ARPPIS programme has managed to operate.

- *Third*, the ICIPE Graduate School could act as a model for Ph.D. training in other major areas of scientific concern in Africa, wherever an advanced centre of R&D emerges on the continent in the near future.

The present Belagio International Conference has come at a most timely juncture in Africa's development history. We pay special homage to those persons and institutions that have actively encouraged us to steer our thinking and planning to a productive goal. These include the Rockefeller Foundation, UNESCO, the Participating Universities in ARPPIS, the regular donors of ARPPIS, the Economic Commission for Africa, the Organization of African Unity, and the Association of African Universities.

KEYNOTE ADDRESS

L.K.H. Goma
*Minister of Higher Education,
Science and Technology
Republic of Zambia*

It is a great honour and privilege to me to have been invited to deliver a Keynote Address at the Inaugural Session of this important Conference. I also wish, at this juncture, to express the sincere gratitude of all of us — the participants — to the Rockefeller Foundation and the International Centre of Insect Physiology and Ecology (ICIPE) for bringing us together in these idyllic surroundings. At the same time, tribute must also go to the insects and the cause of education for this event.

Capacity Building and Human Resource Development

The twin issues of capacity building and human resource development are now the 'in-thing' when considering any long-term development strategy for African countries, as indeed, for those elsewhere in the developing world. The building of indigenous African skills, knowledge and institutions is increasingly and more seriously recognised even by key international bodies like the World Bank and the International Monetary Fund as being of central importance to sustainable development. Some of the recent highlights of this recognition include the Roundtable on Capacity Building and Human Resource Development in Africa, convened by the Lester Pearson Institute for International Development, Dalhousie University, Halifax, Nova Scotia, Canada, in September, 1989; the establishment of the African Capacity Building Foundation with the involvement of the World Bank in 1990, and located in Harare, Zimbabwe; and the Roundtable Conference on Operationalising the African Capacity Building Initiative convened by the Lester Pearson Institute for International Development and the African Capacity Building Foundation, in Harare earlier this month.

It must be stated, though, that these issues have been the subject of debate for a long time which has sometimes been complicated or enriched by the differing and changing attitudes of governments and certain international financial institutions. The positive resurgence of interest in these issues by international organisations and aid agencies is, therefore, most welcome.

There can be no doubt that policy analysis and development management require solid indigenous leadership. Regrettably, there is still considerable reliance on and use of so-called foreign experts in many African countries. Vast amounts of financial resources are locked up in meeting the cost of recruiting, salaries and certain conditions of service, and repatriation of these experts; as a consequence, frequently not much of the donor aid package is ploughed into the capacity-building endeavour or the development of the much-needed local human resources to replace the alien.

Although the climate with regard to the imperative of capacity building and human resource development is now more favourable than before, the question must still be asked: where is the 'building' and the 'development' to be done most effectively? I will come back to this later on.

There is a Hole in the Bucket

The blistering winds of stringency blowing unabated across the African continent have had and continue to have devastating consequences for higher education in most African countries, leaving in their wake many universities broken and weakened. This has heightened the complex problems of decadence, isolation, ineffective utilisation of resources, brain drain and retreat from the 'Knowledge Frontier' afflicting these institutions.

The existence of these problems affects the task of capacity building and human resource development in Africa in various ways. Thus, the inability to sustain excellence in the work done, the isolation of the scientist or scholar from vibrant current development in his field elsewhere, the retreat from the 'Knowledge Frontier, as demonstrated by the abandonment of research work (and consequently, of the genuine cultivation and advancement of knowledge), or by the existence of weak research efforts and lack of solid achievements in the endeavour — these, separately or together, have a negative impact on the quest of building institutions as respected centres of excellence in specific areas; on the progress of science and scholarship in our countries; on the kind and quality of individual academic/professional work; and on the teaching and training of students. Failure to produce competent graduates (or graduates of an unambiguous integrity) means failure to overcome the debilitating shortage of that high-level manpower that African countries badly need for their development and progress. Inadequate funding of institutions results in ineffective utilisation of the available resources, both human and material; it is central to the 'brain drain' which deprives both institutions and countries of the much-needed local expertise and quality human resources; and it is an impediment to the development and/or sustaining of viable postgraduate programmes at many of our universities.

Under these circumstances, the contribution of many of our universities and other institutions of higher learning to the task of capacity building and human resource development has become difficult to fulfil. It is clear that there is a hole in the capacity-building and human resource development 'bucket': as attempts have been made to fill it up, the contents have oozed and continue to ooze out, thus perpetuating the glaring inadequacies in essential indigenous African capacities — institutions, skills and knowledge. This hole must be plugged.

Getting Rid of the Albatross About the Neck

In describing his agonising experience, the Ancient Mariner, in the poem by Samuel Taylor Coleridge, says:

> "Instead of the cross, the Albatross
> About my neck was hung".

This can be likened to the stranglehold of inherited traditions in Africa with respect to attempts at some new and alternative approaches to capacity building and human resource development, especially in the case of postgraduate studies. As a consequence, the advancement of science and scholarship suffers.

There are some people who refuse to accept the possibility of postgraduate education and training being offered by and done entirely at institutions other than universities. There are others who even now still believe that postgraduate studies for Africans can best be done overseas. That is why the comment in the background to the agenda for this conference is so pertinent: "The broadening of the capacity development base by the involvement of research institutes and similar centres of excellence in education is a relatively novel idea in Africa and has not been embraced without some doubt and contention". Although it has not been easy, we must persevere with the fight to remove the frustration of innovative approaches in this direction.

It is and should be a matter of great concern to us that, as observed by the World Bank, "A new spectrum of scientific and technological knowledge is unfolding outside the African continent". Nevertheless, we must recognise the fact that the ICIPE is a leading research institute in Insect Science in the pan-tropical region. Because of its steadfast deployment at the 'Knowledge Frontier', it should be enabled to continue to provide leadership in Insect Science in Africa through research and involvement in postgraduate education and training.

Such involvement is not and should not be considered to be in competition with, but rather as complementing, the work of universities. The goal is to exploit the opportunities offered by the ICIPE. The Graduate School idea is intended to build on a proud record of innovation and achievement in postgraduate education and training at the ICIPE. A degree-awarding Graduate School, concentrating on Ph.D. programmes, will provide a stable framework for the realisation of the ICIPE mandate for training.

As we approach the twenty-first century, Africa is still weak in providing opportunities for postgraduate education and training. But this is because most people look at this in the 'traditional' manner of doing things. We need to break out of the traditional mould. The African Regional Postgraduate Programme in Insect Science (ARPPIS) at ICIPE has shown the way.

I, therefore, hope that this Conference will give strong support to the two issues which the Director of the ICIPE has indicated the institution is putting forward:

- the idea of an ICIPE Graduate School in Insect Science; and
- the notion of Graduate Schools in specialised areas being attached to advanced centres of research so as to expedite capacity building in Africa with a relevant research and intellectual environment.

Bellagio I in 1981, which resulted in the establishment of the ARPPIS, was an act of courage. Bellagio II in 1991 would be an act of even greater courage to rid us of the albatross about the neck.

I wish the Conference every success.

THE ROLE OF UNESCO IN AFRICAN SCIENCE

Adnan Badran
*Assistant Director-General for Science
United Nations Educational, Scientific and
Cultural Organisation (UNESCO)
Paris, France*

The UNESCO Regional Office for Science and Technology in Africa (ROSTA)

BACKGROUND

The General Conference of UNESCO at its thirteenth session in 1964, "with a view to making more effective, UNESCO's contribution to Member States in the development of their science programmes, particularly in the application of science and technology to development", authorised the Director-General, under Resolution 2.342, "to maintain the science cooperation offices and to establish, for the present, one Regional Centre for Science and Technology in Africa".

The activities of ROSTA cover 45 Member States in the African Region. Considering the vast area covered by ROSTA and especially to assist the Office to carry out its mandate more effectively, the "Dakar Unit of ROSTA" was established and based at the Regional Office for Education in Africa (BREDA), Dakar, Senegal, to operate as a separate office unit under the professional responsibility of the head office in Nairobi.

MANDATE

The mandate of the Office, since its inception, has undergone a number of modifications which have taken into account the dynamics of change, and the evolving functions of UNESCO programmes. These have increasingly emphasised scientific and technological education and training in order to meet the socio-economic needs of Member States.

Regional Programmes: Participation in the preparation, planning, execution and evaluation of the Organisation's regional programmes in science and technology, whether financed under the Regular Programme or from extra-budgetary sources.

Advisory Services: In liaison with Headquarters, the Regional Office provides advisory services to Member States at their request, on scientific and technological matters of a national character. With this in view, the Regional Office will maintain contact and collaboration with the national authorities responsible for policy-making in science and technology.

Training of Personnel: In collaboration with Headquarters, the Regional Office will organise training courses, symposia and seminars devoted to scientific and technological subjects of interest to the countries in the region.

Inter-governmental Meetings: The Regional Office will participate in the preparation and follow-up of conferences of ministers and government experts responsible for science and technology.

Studies and Research: The Regional Office will collect available information and undertake studies in the countries in the region which will help Member States to establish and carry out scientific and technologial projects.

Support for Operational Programmes: In pursuance of the decentralisation policy, the Regional Office with the assistance of Headquarters (the Operational Programmes Division in particular), will cooperate with Member States for country programming, the preparation of projects and the evaluation of the results achieved. The Regional Office will help the various technical assistance experts in their work by taking part in inspection missions and participating in the general guidance, supervision and coordination of operational projects in the region.

SCIENTIFIC ACTIVITIES

The scientific activities of the Office have been arranged taking into account the various scientific divisions at UNESCO Headquarters, and have been organised as follows:

Science and Technology Policies
- Coordinate country programming in the region.

- Prepare and execute scientific programmes and activities under UNDP and Funds-in-Trust agreements with UNESCO.
- Assist Member States in the region in determining their scientific and technological needs and in particular, in determining suitable scientific policies and working machineries in their respective countries.
- Follow up activities in respective Member States, arising from recommendations of CASTAFRICA.

Basic Sciences and Scientific Information

- Maintain working contacts with governmental and non-governmental national and regional scientific and technological organisations, reseach institutions and universitites to achieve efficient planning and execution of UNESCO's programmes in basic sciences, science and technology policy and general information.
- Promote teaching, training, research and information-sharing acitivities in the chemical, biological, physical, mathematical and computer sciences.

Technological Research and Training

- Promote international cooperation in research and development in priority fields of engineering sciences.
- Stimulate and encourage activities connected with regional cooperation and the establishment of national research and training infrastructure in the engineering and technical institutes, in particular those leading to the solution of problems arising from choice of appropriate technologies.

Ecology and Environmental Programmes

- Promote and develop programmes and activities in the ecological sciences, natural resources management and environmental education.
- Liaise with the locally-based United Nations Environment Programme (UNEP) in Nairobi.
- Promote MAB activities, particularly the establishment of national committees.

Water Sciences

- Promote acitivities related to the problems and development of hydrology and water resources in the region.
- Promote activities related to the International Hydrology Programme (IHP) in respective countries.

Earth Sciences

- Assist African specialists' involvement in UNESCO's global International Geological Correlation Progamme (IGCP).
- Contact institutions in the region, where research development explorations for minerals, classification of soils and geological surveys are taking place.

Marine Sciences

- Promote marine sciences at the national and regional levels through the development of manpower, infrastructure and research. This entails strengthening of university teaching programmes and marine research laboratories and developing sound scientific research programmes.
- Assist African specialists' participation in the global and regional programmes of the Intergovernmental Oceanographic Commission (IOC) of UNESCO.

PROJECT ACTIVITIES SUPERVISED BY ROSTA

The Office has also maintained a supervisory role in respect to the following project facilities:

- the Turkana Resources Evaluation Monitoring Unit (TREMU)
- the African Network of Scientific and Tecnological Institutions (ANSTI)
- UNESCO/UNFPA Regional Project in Population Communication
- UNESCO/UNFPA Project on Population Education
- UNESCO/UNFPA Population Communication
- Mombasa Conservation Project
- Kenya Population/Mass Media Campaign
- Population and Family Life Education Project

NON-SCIENTIFIC PROGRAMMES

In addition to carrying out the above mandate, the Office also caters for regional programmes in fields other than science and technology, this being a logical consequence of the growth in the role and effectiveness of the Office which foresaw its development as an integrated multi-disciplinary entity. Activities of a non-scientific nature which come under the administrative and supervisory responsibility of ROSTA, but which fall under the sectors of UNESCO other than the scientific sector are: the Office of the Regional Communication Adviser for East and Southern Africa; the Regional Population Communication Unit; the UNESCO/UNICEF Cooperative

Programme in Basic Education for Eastern Africa; and the UNESCO Programme of Cooperation with UNHCR for assistance to refugees in Eastern Africa.

ESTABLISHMENT OF AFSAU

Apart from activities undertaken in conjunction with Headquarters and Member States, the Office has made other notable achievements in recent years. These include the establishment of the Association of Faculties of Science in African Universities (AFSAU) and the initiation of related research and training activities in various scientific disciplines. The Office has also been responsible for the creation of a programme of African Network of Scientific and Technological Institutions (ANSTI) in the region, being currently supported by funds provided by UNDP and Germany.

Postgraduate Training Through the ANSTI Project

Over the years UNESCO has assisted many African countries in developing their universities and engineering schools by the provision of experts to advise on curricula and the development of infrastructure such as classrooms, laboratories, workshops, the preparation of inventories of the equipment, machines and other material required for the proper functioning of these schools. The training of teaching and technicial staff has also been a priority.

The teaching of basic sciences and engineering in these countries at the undergraduate level has thus been more or less consolidated, and in many schools emphasis is now being put on the development of the effectiveness of the teaching staff as well as on research related to local needs. Basic science departments and engineering schools which are united within the framework of the African Network of Scientific and Technological Institutions (ANSTI) are now cooperating in drawing up postgraduate training courses that relate directly to the societal needs of the continent. For example, within this project several hundreds of scientific and engineering staff belonging to more than 40 engineering departments in more than 30 African countries have received various forms of training in research and postgraduate studies. The training activities have been undertaken through the exchange of academic staff, the exchange of students and the award of fellowships, the organisation of continuing education workshops and the support to staff for the acquisition of practical skills in industry and advanced laboratories. In all, thirteen disciplinary sub-networks in engineering and basic science have been established in the following fields:

- agricultural engineering and food processing technology; chemical engineering; civil engineering; electrical and electronic engineering; energy (solar and unconventional power sources); mechanical engineering; metallurgical engineering; mining and geological engineering; water resources and environmental engineering; chemistry; earth sciences; mathematics and statistics; physics.

Furthermore, many training courses in problem areas such as renewable energy, use of improved local building materials, metrology and improvement of traditional technologies for rural development, have been mounted by UNESCO to supplement the disciplinary activities carried out through the ANSTI project.

The Ecological Sciences in Africa

In Africa, ecology as a scientific discipline is not as far developed as in the industrialised countries. Some authors have made a point that this is due to the fact that most African societies are still largely rural societies for which the natural environment can pose serious threats in terms of droughts, floods, dangers of wildlife, tropical diseases, etc. Their aim is therefore much more geared towards developing into urban societies with the amenities that city life can offer. Industrialised countries, on the other hand, which have experienced city life since the Industrial Revolution are much more inclined towards a "Back to Nature" tendency and have therefore developed ecology to better understand the functioning of ecosystems with a view to restoring degraded environments and to making better use of existing natural resources.

Rapid urbanisation processes in Africa since the Second World War coupled with high population growth in rural African areas and the depletion of natural resources indicate that Africa will eventually follow the pattern of the countries in the northern hemisphere. It is therefore necessary to provide Africa now with specialists in ecology to counteract environmental degradation. Improving the rational use of natural resources should be at the heart of socio-economic development programmes for Africa before it is too late. Here, administrative, institutional, political and economic constraints are often considered as obstacles to improving the natural resource uses. Inadequate qualitative and quantitative information on the functioning of ecosystems, the rational utilisation of natural resources and lack of qualified ecological scientists further complicate the situtation in Africa.

MAN AND THE BIOSPHERE PROGRAMME

UNESCO's Programme on Man and the Biosphere (MAB) wishes to assist African countries in strengthening their scientific research capacities on environmental matters. The Programme aims at disseminating information on research results emanating from specific environmental studies which can be used in similar bioclimatic zones with similar prevailing environmental problems. This is achieved by publishing and diffusing scientific literature or by convening international conferences to bring together scientists from all over the world for exchange of ideas and expertise. Moreover, MAB is actively engaged in training scientists at all levels: through organising workshops, through arranging of study tours and study programmes, and through awarding research grants to young scientists for activities within the framework of the MAB Programme.

The MAB Programme is trying to overcome information gaps and scientific capacity deficits by implementing environmental research projects in many developing countries, and in particular in Africa. These projects offer the advantages that African scientists can work on specific environmental issues, they can use existing methodologies or develop their own methodologies and younger graduate and postgraduate scientists can receive training through on-the-job research work. MAB research projects are usually of a duration of two to five years and favour holistic and integrated approaches to problem-solving through interdisciplinary (natural and social sciences) research work.

Presently, African MAB field projects are located in the tropical forest zone and in semi-arid and arid lands. For example, the project "Strengthening of Scientific Capacities in the Field of Agro-silvo-pastoral Management in the Sahelian Countries" aims at reinforcing cooperation between research and development institutions for better valorising research activities and results in this field. The project also includes scientific and technical information exchanges on various activities of rural development aspects and combating desertification in the Sahel. The project builds on the experience of a former project — FAPIS — which has been implemented by UNESCO for 10 years and which has focused on the training for integrated pastoral management and development in the Sahel.

Another MAB project, the "Turkana Resources Evaluation and Monitoring Unit" in the semi-arid region of north-western Kenya is concerned with livestock and vegetation studies to elaborate management guidelines for improved cattle grazing in collaboration with the Turkana nomads. This project also draws on the experiences and results gained during the "Integrated Project on Arid Lands (IPAL)" in Kenya which studied the complex inter-relationships existing between population increase, socio-economic changes, partial sedentarisation, over-grazing, and desertification.

It would lead too far to mention all the MAB projects in Africa — more detailed information on our projects can be obtained from the international MAB Secretariat at UNESCO Headquarters.

BIOSPHERE RESERVES

Let me focus briefly on a special feature of the MAB Programme which can be considered as a new approach for protecting the environment, applying practical field research, providing training, and integrating indigenous populations in all these activities. I am referring here to Biosphere Reserves. Today there are 300 reserves in 75 countries representing approximately two-thirds of all terrestrial regions of the world. Biosphere reserves are protected areas of representative ecosystems that have been recognised by MAB for their value in providing scientific knowledge, skills and human values needed to support sustainable development. They are valuable models for sustainable development as they help to conserve biological resources, perpetuate traditional forms of land use, monitor natural and social changes, and improve the overall management of natural resources. Wherever possible, biosphere reserves are used as sites for comparative studies and international pilot projects.

Capacity Building in Marine Sciences in Africa

"Africa needs science, not just technology" — is the statement by Prof. Thomas Odhiambo, President of the African Academy of Sciences (from the *New Scientist* - November 1990). UNESCO's marine science programmes (COMAR, PROMAR, TREDMAR) are strongly oriented to research capacity-building in developing countries, through imple-mentation of various activities financed both from the UNESCO regular budget and extra-budgetary sources (UNDP, World Bank, UNEP, etc.).

The African Coastal Marine project (COMARAF) (1988-1991) is an example of important UNDP/UNESCO input in research capacity development in Africa.

A concern has been voiced by an increased number of African coastal countries regarding the need for scientific information on which to base future management decisions. COMARAF is a response to this concern, being a regional component of UNESCO's Major Interregional Coastal Marine project (COMAR). Its purpose is to organise and carry out a multi-disciplinary study of the African marine coastal zone, a study which contributes to the scientific basis for decision-makers in planning the sustainable development of their countries. Specifically, the project is investigating the decline of natural balances that characterise the coastal marine systems. Further, the COMARAF strengthens the scientific infrastructure and management capacity of the participating countries (now 15 in number) through appropriate training, research and dissemination of information.

Between 1988-91, COMARAF implemented three training courses and nine research methodology workshops, which involved over 200 researchers and technicians from 15 countries of Africa. A number of individual fellowships and study grants were granted, to effect advanced training outside the region as well as (VERY IMPORTANT!) in the region, using existing research and training capacities in advanced laboratories/universities. The general approach of the project is to bring together existing research forces and capacities (laboratories, equipment, etc.) in order to create multiplying effects at the regional level.

By now, within the COMARAF project 11 documents have been published, reflecting results of joint efforts of African scientists to study the most critical environmental fringe: the coastal zone.

The Biosciences in Africa

The Hon. F.K. Buah, Minister of Education, Republic of Ghana, in his opening remarks on the occasion of the UNESCO/ICSU Symposium on the "State of Biology in Africa" that took place at Accra in April 1981, said:

> "The Accra Symposium of the International Biosciences Network (IBN), I understand, is another milestone in the formation of such networks in various regions of the world, with the express purpose of opening up and exploiting areas of biological research of particular promise and relevance to the needs of developing countries, thanks to the coordinated efforts of the International Council of Scientific Unions (ICSU); the United Nations Educational, Scientific and Cultural Organisation (UNESCO), and the United Nations Development Programme (UNDP)."

A direct outcome of the Accra Symposium was the establishment of the African Biosciences Network (ABN). In 1981 a Regional Executive Committee for the ABN was set up following the Accra Symposium, and all African countries were invited to set up National ABN Committees of scientists.

THE AFRICAN BIOSCIENCES NETWORK (ABN)

The African Biosciences Network is a cooperative mechanism linking biological institutions and bioscientists in sub-Saharan Africa in a common effort aimed at improving the level of know-how and the applications of the biological sciences throughout the region. The ABN is the African regional arm of the International Biosciences Network (IBN), through which the expertise of the international scientific community is brought into close contact with the African Network.

The principal objectives of the ABN are to support bioscientists and to strengthen existing institutions throughout the region so that they are better able to undertake their research in the basic biological sciences and in finding solutions to the pressing problems of a biological nature confronting the region. In order to consolidate their programme, the scientists participating in the ABN have agreed that their efforts could be focused on the priority areas of food production and health.

The ABN achieves its objectives through a process which allows African scientists themselves to identify the problems they need to study, and to organise relevant research and/or training activities aimed at resolving these problems. The ABN also organises scientific meetings on specific topics, and arranges for the preparation and dissemination of scientific publications, resulting from its own activities, or focusing on a key problem to be resolved.

MICROBIAL BIOTECHNOLOGY

Microbial biotechnology offers the developing countries great scope for progress since most of the resources and conditions needed for its use exist in these countries. Furthermore, it is a field that calls for regional and international cooperation as it has applications in the fields of agriculture, industry, engineering, the environment, medicine and overall national development. Taking into account the possibilities to develop endogenous capacities for the strengthening of existing research infrastructures, and as a follow-up to the recommendations of the CASTAFRICA* (Dakar, 1974) and CASTARAB* (Rabat, 1976) Conferences and the U.N. Conference on Science and Technology for Development (UNCSTD), Vienna, 1980, UNESCO initiated a major regional project for Africa and the Arab States in the field of applied microbiology and biotechnology in 1981.

The rationale of the project which came to an end in 1986 was to develop the research potential and technological capacity already existing in these countries through promotion of scientific cooperation between existing local institutions and regional professional societies within the framework of the regional networks of microbial resources centres (MIRCENs), especially through the MIRCENs for East and West Africa at the University of Nairobi and the Centre National de Recherches Agronomiques de Bambey, Senegal and for the Arab States at the Ain Shams University, Cairo, Egypt.

This project, through implementation, attempted to promote high-value, low-cost technologies that improve rural agricultural practices, create rural market economies and provide more technological avenues for employment, increased incomes and ultimate feeder industries to the urban sector.

BIOSCIENCE AND BIOTECHNOLOGY TRANSFER AND DEVELOPMENT

Africa, still the victim of hunger, famine, disease and poverty, poses a challenge in this final decade of the century that ends with the emphasis on sustainable development. The continent's available resources are not used efficiently to generate socio-economic progress. The development of biotechnologies has opened up new prospects for agriculture, health, chemical and pharmaceutical industries, energy, and the protection of the environment, and at the same time has become an area of keen international competition. One may query whether biotechnologies will help to solve some of the socio-economic problems of Africa or, will widen further the gap between North and South. The developing countries in Africa cannot remain on the fringe of basic biological research and its technological applications, especially as in many fields these can be utilised with moderate outlay by turning to natural resources. Along with the advantages, there are constraints associated with the practical utilisation of biotechnologies and it is therefore advisable to define appropriate policies in order to benefit from them. Some of these issues were addressed in the First Congress of African Scientists that was organised by the Organisation of African Unity, UNDP and UNESCO at Brazzaville, Congo, June 1987.

The choice, transfer and adaptation of biotechnologies and the biosciences deserve special attention, so as to introduce technological systems adapted to the economic, social and cultural conditions of African countries. Solutions will differ in tropical humid and dry zones, and in rural and industrial societies. It is, therefore, better for the developing countries to adopt and develop to the appropriate level, low-cost, effective biotechnologies, easily transferred and adapted to local conditions. However, every national scientific and technological community must also, where possible, utilise more sophisticated techniques, or adapt them to build up projects, in order to meet local needs and to keep abreast of biotechnological developments internationally. Every country should draw up a list of priorities so as to derive maximum benefit from the resources available.

Of all the prerequisites, the most crucial for Africa is that of human competence. Assimilation of biotechnologies and of the biosciences will have to rely on experienced people. This pre-supposes a sufficiently open, multi-disciplinary training for future biotechnologists which could be achieved through research and training programmes led jointly by the African and the industrialised countries, adapted to local conditions and needs.

The Natural Sciences Sector Programme and Budget for the Biennium 1992-1993 (Draft 26C/S)

The two overall priorities of the science sector as a whole for the biennium 1992-1993 are the environmental sciences and the basic sciences, as shown in Figure 1.

FIGURE 1: PRIORITIES OF THE NATURAL SCIENCES SECTOR, 1992-1993

	Overall Priority Intentions of Whole Sector
First:	Environment
Second:	Basic Sciences
	Concentration Areas Per Sub-Programme
Basic sciences:	University teaching at all levels; research networks.
Engineering:	University teaching at all levels. R&D in environmentally sound technologies.
Coordinated global programmes:	Global change and sustainable development; UNCED.
Geology:	Geological correlation, IGCP; geology for environmentally sound development.
Natural hazards:	Natural geological hazards, IDNDR.
Ecology:	Biological diversity, biosphere reserves, MAB, Natural World Heritage.
Oceanography:	Ocean observing and monitoring systems; coastal marine systems, training, IOC/MRI.
Hydrology:	Eco-hydrology. Climate change impacts, IHP.
S&T Culture:	Popularisation of science.
S&T Management:	Advice and training on management of S&T.
Co-operation for development:	Project identification, design, formulation, monitoring and evaluation.

Within the Natural Sciences Sector, direct programme costs total US$ 22.5m, of which 39% has been allocated for science and technology development. Of this $ 8.75m, about $ 5.5m (63%) is available for basic sciences research, as shown below in Table 1.

TABLE 1: UNESCO NATURAL SCIENCES SECTOR

Science and Technology: Direct Programme Costs

AREA	US$	%
Basic sciences research	5,498,200	62.8
Engineering cooperation	941,800	10.8
Science, university and industry relations	196,000	2.2
Basic sciences teaching	978,000	11.2
Engineering teaching	1,139,000	13.0
Total	8,753,000	100.0

Of the US $ 52.4m in extra-budgetary funds available, 14.5% (equivalent to $ 7.6m) has been apportioned to the basic sciences and another 24% ($ 12.6m) to the ecological sciences.

One feature of the 1992-93 plan is the further decentralisation of programme activities and staff to the regions (39% of the total staff). Of the decentralised staff, 24% are based in Africa.

INNOVATIVE APPROACHES FOR SUSTAINABLE BUILDING FOR INSECT SCIENCE LEADERSHIP IN AFRICA

M.T. Mapuranga
Assistant Secretary-General
Organisation of African Unity

Introduction

The Organisation of African Unity is grateful to ICIPE for associating it in this important forum. As is well known, the primary preoccupation of the OAU since its inception has been the decolonisation and political emancipation of the Continent.

With the independence of Namibia and signs that the odious system of apartheid in South Africa may be approaching its demise, the OAU is shifting its focus to the economic development of the Continent. On 3rd June 1991 in Abuja, Nigeria, African Heads of State and Government, meeting in their 27th Summit Conference, signed the treaty establishing the African Economic Community, which is designed to be the institutional framework for the economic integration and development of Africa.

Economic Impact of Insect Pests in Africa

It is not difficult to discern that the study of insects or insect science is a subject of great importance to the OAU because it focuses on a major constraint responsible for the shortfall in food production in Africa. Food production and security are fundamental to Africa's attempt at economic development.

Africa is caught in a paradox. Insects are part of the African paradox in that Africa is at once both rich and poor. Africa is rich in people, culture and natural resources, including the creatures of the Animal Kingdom such as insects. The Continent is endowed with diverse ecological zones and has a great agricultural potential. And yet Africa has the greatest food deficit of all the developing regions in the world.

During the 1970s, Africa's agricultural output was on the decline and insect pests were responsible for part of that decline. In the recent past some countries in North

Africa and in the Sahel belt were plagued by swarms of locusts which destroyed crops. Ticks and tick-borne diseases and tsetse fly-transmitted *nagana* (animal trypanosomiasis) have for a long time been major constraints to livestock production in Africa. A number of insect pests have been responsible for the destruction of crops in the fields and other pests for enormous post-harvest losses.

The human population has not been spared either. Malaria parasites transmitted by mosquitoes are responsible for high mortalities, especially among the children of Africa. It is estimated that up to a million children die of malaria in Africa annually. Oncocerciasis, or river blindness, transmitted by sandflies or blackflies, is rampant in some West African countries. Rift Valley Fever, transmitted by mosquitoes, is a serious disease in sheep and cattle and also affects man. Lumpy skin disease, which is also transmitted by insects, is a serious disease affecting cattle in some African countries. The New World screw-worm fly infestation could be disastrous for both human beings and livestock if it extended outside its present locus in Libya. These are only a few examples of the numerous diseases of man and livestock in Africa which are transmitted by insects.

Education in Insect Science

It is quite evident that, for its survival and development, Africa must take innovative approaches to overcome such insect-related problems through the application of science and technology.

Initially, the study of insects or entomology, as it is called, was carried out at African universities with the traditional approach to classical entomology. As we know, a university's primary obligation is the teaching of the undergraduate students. Some universities were able to carry out research, but most of the research results were not sufficiently adapted to the local conditions and environment, and therefore remained in the archives.

Around the time when many African countries attained their independence, numerous national research institutes and programmes were established. These should have formed the backbone of a strong and coherent scientific community. Instead, these have become small, fragile and non-viable national scientific establishments. This has led to the deterioration of scientific and research infrastructure at a time when it is badly needed. As a result we are witnessing poor research management, institutional instability, grossly inadequate funding, and limited relevance of research programmes to national goals. This is partly a function of the absence of a clear policy on science and technology, and partly a function of the severe economic recession that Africa now finds itself in.

In order to improve Africa's scientific and technological development, African countries must pool their resources together. What can we do? Let us learn a lesson from those insects themselves in their hives and their nests. Let us work together.

This approach would make it possible for regional research centres to be established and flourish. Hopefully these would attract adequate financial support from donors and governments and eventually become centres of excellence.

Adequate government financial support should also be given to the science departments at the universities in order to improve their research capabilities and output. After all, both scientists and political leaders share the same objective, i.e., to improve the welfare of the people. The latter should therefore give the former all the requisite support.

If enough resources were made available to both the regional research institutes and the national universities, these establishments would be able to train a critical mass of local insect scientists who could tackle Africa's agricultural and health problems. These scientists must in turn do research in areas of relevance to Africa, and on specific issues which are of medium- and long-term benefit to the Continent.

Research-Extension Linkages

We in the OAU believe that the new insect science technologies to be developed should be geared to the rural population as the main users. After all, over 90% of Africa's people live in the rural areas. Extension services should be sufficiently developed in order to transfer new research results right down to the rural population. Weak extension services, or non-existent research extension linkages, are some of the factors constraining the use of new agricultural technologies.

In order for Africa to move forward, it must acquire science and technology, but the technology must be appropriate to the environment and local needs. For example, it would be a mistake to fight against pests which harm food crops and animals with chemicals which destroy the environment and drain away foreign exchange. Yet at one time there seemed to be no alternative to chemicals. But today we know that biological methods of pest control can do the job while sparing Africa from further environmental damage. The use of traps against tsetse fly infestation, for example, is gradually replacing the massive aerial spraying of insecticides.

In order for Africa to acquire a sustainable capacity and leadership in insect science, it must train a critical mass of high-level scientists. Again, the most practical approach is a combined effort at the regional level.

A sufficient number of middle-level scientists and extension workers must also be trained so that the research findings by the top-level scientists can percolate down to the end-users, the rural population.

Role of the OAU

In conclusion, I would like to state that the OAU has a role to play in the entire exercise. For the regional approach to be effective, the OAU should take a leading role by passing practical or implementable resolutions at the OAU Summit of Heads of State and Government in the area of science and technology. These resolutions would then be implemented by the OAU's Scientific and Technical and Research Commission in collaboration with national institutes responsible for science and technology. Let me conclude by calling upon your expertise to suggest and recommend those practical solutions for consideration and possible adoption by the OAU policy organs.

HIGHER EDUCATION IN AFRICA IN THE LAST THREE DECADES: A DEMOGRAPHIC OVERVIEW

S.H. Ominde
Institute of Population Studies
Nairobi, Kenya

Introduction

The trauma of the last three decades has left the international community with a number of areas of unresolved problems. In no other area are these problems more pressing than in education, because of its central and vital role in the development process. It is also important to note the highest priority accorded by the emergent African political leadership to education, not merely as a necessary preparation of a useful individual in society, but also as a right. This observation is in conflict with the elitist approach to higher education in many of the Western developed countries.

Historically, initial efforts in education are rooted in the changing philosophy of political, social and economic development. It is the late nationalist leader Kwame Nkurumah who is reputed to have popularised the slogan of "Seek ye first the kingdom of politics and the rest shall be added unto you". The initial static phase that stamped the literary character on our education system arose when the early colonial authorities produced what they needed in terms of manufactured goods in metropolitan countries and exploited only the resources and cheap manpower of the African region. With the beginning of the 'wind of change', colonial educational planning entered a new phase, the phase that produced those of us who returned from higher institutions abroad to staff the colonial models of higher education institutions that were being established.

The colonial models of higher education were copies of metropolitan models with standards strictly maintained in accordance with the elitist roots of higher education. We in East and West Africa are familiar with the 'special relationship' institutional arrangements with the University of London and stringent admission regulations that kept university enrolment unrealistically small. It was also unrealistically small because there was still plenty of unused capacity in metropolitan universities that could accommodate the small numbers qualifying from colonial educational institutions. However, the real problem was that in the absence of a clear demographic base, colonial higher education models were soon out of step with the rising demand for higher education. This rising demand was fueled by the strong nationalism associated with independence movements.

With this brief introduction, I propose first to examine the demographic context of higher education development. The objective here is to demonstrate that some of the crises of higher education have been due to our persistence in ignoring the interplay between demographic pressures and the nature of higher education problems. These issues dovetail with the ever-changing problems of Africa's development in a world which is not keen in eliminating the gross inequalities that hamper the region's participation in building a better world. I will then examine the nature of the human resource crisis and the problems of science and technology in meeting Africa's needs. This will also open a brief examination of important changes in attitude of some of the more developed countries towards access to higher education institutions. Finally, I will examine the options of science and technology in Africa in the 21st century. I propose to conclude by examining the critical role of an ICIPE model and its contribution to the network concept in the future development of facilities for higher education.

Demographic Context of Higher Education Development in Africa

DEMOGRAPHIC TRENDS FROM 1950-2020

Africa, christened the *Dark Continent* for centuries, remained a mystery to science with its inseparable foundation on scientific data. It was not until the middle of World War II that demographic prospects in Africa began to dawn on the conscience of scientists. Students of demography had not only to contend with the lack of data but also with the insoluble problem of whether conclusions derived from years of census experience in Europe and elsewhere could be applied in Africa. It is in these circumstances that the first post-World War II Kenya Education Commission, chaired by the late Leonard Beecher, published a report with educational demographic statistics drawn from the British experience in Britain.

Given the imperfections of population data on a global scale, Africa's population trend over this period is a microcosm of the global population trends beginning with the middle of the 20th century. The acceleration of Africa's population, which now ranks the region at the top of the growth rate ladder, is in itself the result of the impact of science and technology emanating from the more developed world. Table 1 shows the global trends in population between 1950 and 1977 as compared to major world regions and Table 2 shows the situation among various regions of Africa. This period covers the most critical part of the region's population growth.

TABLE 1: WORLD POPULATION AND AVERAGE ANNUAL RATES OF GROWTH 1950-1977

Mid-Year Population (thousands)

Region	1977	1975	1970	1965	1960	1955	1950
World	4,257,655	4,100,271	3,721,518	3,371,239	3,057,737	2,769,606	2,525,852
More developed	1,154,439	1,137,410	1,087,279	1,036,567	975,288	913,389	855,150
Less developed	3,103,216	2,962,861	2,634,239	2,334,672	2,082,449	1,856,213	1,670,702
Africa	430,757	407,368	356,384	313,369	277,011	246,032	222,039

Average Annual Rate of Growth

Region	1975-77	1970-75	1965-70	1960-65	1955-60	1950-55
World	1.9	1.9	2.0	2.0	2.0	1.8
More developed	0.7	0.9	1.0	1.2	1.3	1.3
Less developed	2.3	2.4	2.4	2.3	2.3	2.1
Africa	2.8	2.7	2.6	2.5	2.3	2.1

Source: *US World Population Trends and Policies*, Vol. 1, Table 2, 1977.

TABLE 2: POPULATION OF AFRICA 1977 AND VITAL RATES BY SUB-REGION

Sub-region	Estimated Population July, 1977 (Thousands)	Births per 1000 Population	Deaths per 1000 Population	Rate of Growth (per cent)
AFRICA	430,757	45-48	18-20	2.5-2.9
Eastern Africa	122,895	40-50	18-20	2.6-3.0
Middle Africa	49,011	43-47	18-22	2.0-2.7
Northern Africa	102,974	44	14-15	2.9-3.0
Southern Africa	30,186	36-38	12-13	2.3-2.5
Western Africa	125,691	48-50	21-24	2.4-2.9

Source: *US World Population 1977, Op cit.* Table A-1, p. 27.

Table 3 shows the various demographic indicators by major regions of the world projected into the 21st century. Table 4 shows that whereas the total population of the less developed regions is expected to increase from 4,107m in mid-1990 to 5,018m in the year 2000 and 6,828m in the year 2020, that of Africa is expected to increase from 611m in mid-1990 to 884m in the year 2000 and 1,481m in the year 2020 A.D. Factors accounting for the indicated trends include sustained high fertility and falling mortality, especially infant mortality over the period in question. The momentum of the growth trends indicated will continue to depend on infant mortality and sustained high fertility, which have been some of the major targets of global, regional and national health policies.

TABLE 3: WORLD DEMOGRAPHIC PROFILE 1990

Africa	Less Developed	More Developed	World	Region or Country
661	4,107	1,214	5,321	Population esimates mid-1990(millions)
44	31	15	27	Birth rate (per 1000) population
15	10	9	10	Death rate (per 1000) population
2.9	2.1	0.5	1.8	Natural rate of increase (annual %)
24	33	128	39	Population doubling time (years) at current rates
884	5,018	1,274	6,292	Population projected to 2000 (millions)
1,481	6,878	1,350	8,228	Population projected to 2020(millions)
109	81	16	73	Infant mortality rate
6.2	4.0	2.0	3.5	Total fertility rate
45/3	36/4	22/12	33/6	% population under age 15/65+
52	61	74	64	Life expectancy at birth (years)
31	32	73	41	Urban population (%)

Source: *Population Reference Bureau, Inc. World Population Data Sheet 1990*, Washington, D.C.

TABLE 4: AFRICA: DEMOGRAPHIC PROFILE 1990-2020

Southern Africa	Middle Africa	Eastern Africa	Western Africa	Northern Africa	Region or Country
45	68	199	206	144	Population estimates mid-1990 (millions)
36	45	47	47	38	Birth rate (per 1000) population
9	16	17	17	10	Death rate (per 1000) population
2.7	3.0	3.0	3.0	2.8	Natural rate of increase (annual %)
26	23	23	23	25	Population doubling time (years) at current rates
59	91	273	279	183	Population projected to 2000 (millions)
95	156	481	481	268	Population projected to 2020 (millions)
61	118	116	119	87	Infant mortality rate
4.7	6.1	6.7	6.6	5.2	Total fertility rate
40/4	45/3	47/3	46/2	43/4	% population under age 15/65+
62	50	50	48	59	Life expectancy at birth (years)
53	37	18	30	41	Urban population(%)

Source: *Population Reference Bureau Inc.: World Population Data Sheet 1990. Washington, D.C.*

All the major sub-regions of Africa are expected to have substantial increases by the end of this century and by the year 2020 A.D. (Table 4). It is this story of accelerated increases in population that lies at the root of many of the acute problems of socio-economic development of the region, including that of higher education. Table 5 shows that, whereas a small decline is expected in the underage population between the years 1980 and 2025 A.D., the proportion of persons aged 15 to 64 years will experience a substantial increase.

TABLE 5: PROJECTED AGE STRUCTURE OF AFRICA MEDIUM VARIANT, SELECTED YEARS 1980-2100 A.D.

Year and Indicator	Africa
1980	
Median Age	17.5
Percent 0-14	44.9
Percent 15-64	52.1
Percent 65+	3.0
Dependency ratio*	92.2
2000	
Median Age	17.8
Percent 0-14	43.9
Percent 15-64	52.9
Percent 65+	3.2
Dependency ratio*	89.0
2025	
Median Age	22.8
Percent 0-14	34.1
Percent 15-64	61.6
Percent 65+	4.3
Dependency ratio*	62.4

*The dependency ratio is the number of persons aged 0-14 and 65 and over per 100 persons aged 15-64. Source: *Population Bulletin of the UN, 1982, No. 14, pp. 25-26.*

This is not the place for an in-depth study of the demographic indicators of population change in the last three decades. It is mentioned in passing to underline the fact that demographic trends must be taken into account in the balance sheet of our development success or failure in higher education.

CHANGING ROLES OF EDUCATION

Quantitatively, most African countries would show impressive increases in enrolment since the first generation of colonial models of higher education were established. These were established at a time when the international climate of opinion considered the self-reliance role of higher education seriously and supported it generously.

However, it is the contention in this paper that the position has drastically changed. African countries faced with the miserable burden of poor economic performance have found higher education as the likely target for severe cuts. The open-ended approach to higher education is being replaced with such slogans as "cost sharing" as pressure mounts in the basic sectors of primary and secondary school education. The current Kenya Development Plan 1989-1993 underscores the problem in the following terms:

> "In spite of the considerable achievement Kenya has made in the area of education... two significant issues have emerged that will require to be given serious consideration during the Plan period. These relate to the relevance of education system to the changing needs of the economy and the cost of education.[1]"

The current Kenya National Development Plan stresses that the guiding philosophy on education is that in general, the education system should aim at producing individuals who are properly socialised and who possess the necessary knowledge, skills, attitudes and values to enable them to participate positively in nation-building.[2]

When Mwalimu Julius K. Nyerere published his seminal guiding philosophy on "Education for Self-Reliance" in the mid-1960's, he was trying to make a breakthrough in that area of education that faced the first Kenya National Education Review. The basic challenge of the Review was the creation of a national system of education that satisfied the aspirations of both the majority African as well as the non-African population that Kenya was still cautiously caring for. By virtue of the complexity of the content and objective problems, and the time factor, the Commission was constrained to deal only with the key issues. The recommendation of the Reviews of Education in Kenya extending from 1964 to 1988 have been accepted by the Government.[3] However, even the 1988 Presidential Review that introduced the `8-4-4' system in Kenya was still grappling with this problem of content and relevance.

---

1   Republic of Kenya: Development Plan 1989-1993; para. 9.46, p. 212. Government Printer, Nairobi, 1989.
2   Republic of Kenya: Development Plan 1989-1993. *Op. cit.* para. 9.45, pp. 210-211.
3   Republic of Kenya: Development Plan 1989-1993. *Op. cit.*

The fact of the matter is that educational reform in Kenya, and for that matter in Africa, has had to move slowly due to an inherent conflict in making educational development relevant to the ever-changing national needs with the demographic impact on the quality of education. In this conflict, it is the basic foundations of a science and technological education that has suffered.

THE ECONOMIC ROLE OF EDUCATION

It is the newly emerging economic role of education that poses the real danger to a global interchange of scientific and technological know-how. Knowledge generated in the powerhouses of higher education is no longer considered freely accessible. It is this attitude that compromised the noble aims of the United Nations Conference on Science and Technology when the more developed countries defiantly refused to compromise on the humanitarian need for sharing scientific knowledge, a practice which has been the hall-mark of the international scientific spirit. Some countries even moved decisively to discourage the flow of students from the poorer countries, especially Africa, by charging higher fees.

To the developed countries, knowledge generated in higher education institutions and research institutes has acquired a new dimension. This knowledge is now more and more viewed as part and parcel of continued dominance of the more developed parts of the world over the less developed parts. We now live in a world where computer viruses are a real weapon in interfering with free exchange of information. These are the problems that are emerging at a time when Africa is taking stock of its success or failure in meeting the needs of science and technological manpower.

ESTABLISHING PRIORITIES FOR SCIENCE AND TECHNOLOGY EDUCATION

Africa has so far performed miserably in the training of the actual scientific and technological manpower needed for it to advance in step with the modern world. On the access side, the avenues that formerly existed in the developed world for providing the resources available for assistance to Africa and which are now limited must be considered as part of a general pressure from the population upsurge of the developing world and now Eastern Europe and the former Marxist countries.

However, a more serious problem is one of choice of priority to be accorded in solving the basic problem of Africa's under-development in science and technological education. Previously, the strategy has been to copy some decades or so later what has been happening in the more developed countries. But as the 20th century draws to a close, it is even more imperative for leaders of Africa's educational planning to be more clear on the paths to follow. The vast global diversity of science and the more specific technological developments geared to solve local problems are too vast for impoverished African nations to copy. We therefore need to take stock of our priority areas in the decades that lie ahead.

To be able to see the problem facing the expansion of the university in developing countries of Africa, the Kenyan Projected Enrolment in Education as provided for in the Plan 1989-1993 is illustrated in Table 6. I made the point earlier of the demographic constraint facing the maintenance and improvement of education. The Kenya Government over the past three decades has been seeking solutions to strengthen the requirements of science and technology. These requirements have become prohibitively expensive in the modernising of education.

The basic system of education has been limping along with these acute shortages which must be overcome if science and technological education are to improve. It is this problem that has created a widening gap in the quality of education in the so-called 'harambee schools' which mushroomed in Kenya in the decades following independence. The inherited weaknesses are merely transferred to higher levels of education including the universities. With increasing reliance on *harambee* (communal fund-raising) efforts to improve facilities, further inequalities have appeared in capacities of various schools to maintain the quality of teaching. The inequalities will persist as new technological innovations in new areas of science are incorporated into the curriculum.

TABLE 6: PROJECTED ENROLMENT IN THE KENYA EDUCATION SYSTEM (THOUSANDS)

Level of Education	1988	1989	1990	1991	1992	1993
Primary Schools	5,217	5,400	5,580	5,762	5,945	6,130
Secondary Schools	553	735	758	790	806	812
Vocational and Technical	17.9	19.5	20.4	21.2	22.0	22.9
Special Education	9.4	10.3	11.3	12.5	13.7	15.1
TEACHER TRAINING						
Primary TTC's*	13.1	13.2	13.3	13.4	13.6	13.7
Diploma TTC's	3.8	4.4	5.0	5.8	6.7	7.8
Graduate Teachers	5.5	6.3	6.9	7.5	7.9	8.1
UNIVERSITY EDUCATION						
Undergraduates	26.0	29.9	34.4	39.5	45.5	52.3
Postgraduates	1.9	2.2	2.4	2.7	3.1	3.4
Adult Literacy	274	301	331	364	401	441

*TTC = Teacher Training Colleges.

Source: *Republic of Kenya: National Development Plan 1989-1993*.

In 1963, there were only 151 secondary schools in Kenya, of which 119 were Government—maintained and 32 private. By 1987, these figures had increased to 2,485 of which 635 were Government- maintained, 1,497 harambee and 353 unaided; as a result, the use of facilities and staff has been severely overstretched.[4] The introduction of the '8-4-4' system with its heavy demand on practical curricula caused an overloading which continues to be rightly criticised. The heavy demands are in turn transmitted to higher levels of education.

---

4 Republic of Kenya: National Development Plan. *Op. cit.* p. 217

The fundamental question affecting science and technology is how much basic foundation in such subjects like mathematics, physics, chemistry, biology and environmental sciences should be taught. Taken in conjunction with the heavy teaching loads of staff as a result of the increasing intake of students, the higher education institutions have yet to review the implications.

The Challenges of Science and Technology in Africa in the 21st Century

PROBLEMS FACING HIGHER EDUCATION

We have dwelt at length in this paper on the demographic implications to education in Africa in order to highlight the seriousness of the situation. In our basic conference document, we have been told that the concern for the capacity to produce intellectual talent to sustain scientific and technological development is not unique to Africa alone. However, although science is universal and technology is problem-specific, there is still the need to understand the African dimensions to these problems.

The higher institutions in Africa and the governments in the region face three major related problems if they are to meet the demand for sufficient human resources and facilities capable of propelling Africa into the 21st century as a competent partner in the international move to a science- and technology-oriented development. The problems identified are:

- Setting priorities in the higher education sector at the regional, national and local level, including in the universities.
- Maintenance of a level of excellence in research and teaching as recognised by the intellectual world.
- Management of the university both as a physical entity and as a community of scholars, interacting with policy makers and as users of university-trained material (including human resources).

These are vast problem areas that we cannot develop in depth over a short period of time.

Clearly the acute shortage which characterises the human resource situation in science and technology is how to find ways of attracting and retaining greater numbers of students in these fields. As has been argued in this overview, the problem is both a question of which models of curricula development we adopt and the priorities which must now characterise higher education in Africa. As the experiences of most African countries show, these problems have never been satisfactorily solved, and the difficulties are aggravated by the accelerated population growth. African countries must place their hopes in providing a sound basic foundation for science and technology in schools and institutions of higher education. This priority includes adequate physical facilities, whether located in selected high-quality schools or shared on a network basis.

NEED FOR SCIENCE TRANSFER

Innovation and inventions in the context of African development must rest on a sound foundation of basic sciences and supporting physical facilities. I need to stress that a sound background in basic sciences also applies to the applied sciences. Africa and the rest of the developing world have pursued science activities as if they are marginal in the development process. Few within developing countries appear to stress that for long-term effectiveness, technology transfer must always be accompanied by science transfer, since the science of today is the technology of tomorrow. Even in the more developed regions of the world, new technologies were based on physical, chemical and later biological research. University teaching and industrial research, formerly parallel, have increasingly been combined, and university scientific staff joined industries, especially the electronic and chemical industries. Science in these countries became central to the improvement of industrial and agricultural production and medical services, as well as other fields.

What is needed in Africa is the permeation of science and technology throughout the productive process. The major problems have been attempts to depend on horizontal transfer of technology without the resource base of scientific knowledge and research which have brought about new technologies. For technology to succeed, there is need for effective emergence of a competent scientific or 'critical mass' backed by adequate human resources and infrastructure.

The key subject areas in basic sciences have included physics with its important linkages with material and other sciences; chemistry and the role of chemistry in national development; biology; mathematics; earth sciences and space science. The applied science division includes:

- Mechanical engineering; electrical and electronics engineering; materials science; mining science; energy, fuels, power and transport.
- Agroforestry; biotechnology; agriculture; water and soil resources; nutrition.
- Medical sciences and environmental health.

PRIORITISING RESEARCH

In these critical areas, African countries need to order their priorities within the remainder of the 20th century to generate the 'critical human resources mass' if they are to make an effective effort in closing the widening gap between the region and centres of science and technology in the West. However, the latest reports of the African situation give a rather gloomy picture. African university staff, according to a World Bank Report, indicate that research within their institutions took a downward plunge in the 1980's. As the financial crisis hit tertiary education, research budgets were the first to be severely cut, not to mention availability of teaching (and in some cases examination) material.

The four Kenyan public universities are currently in a crisis with the financing of postgraduate, particularly doctoral, programmes. This stagnation or outright decline in research support to produce future lecturers and researchers will undoubtedly affect Africa's capacity to benefit from a global exchange of knowledge.

Yet new areas of knowledge and technologies are emerging that could be of vital importance to the region. These areas include genetic engineering and other areas of biotechnology essential to plant and animal health. Even in the area of human health and industrial processes, micro-electronics and materials science, African higher education institutions must constantly re-evaluate their programmes and contributions to training and research. The high cost of these new avenues requires that institutions address themselves squarely to the problem of priority rationalisation and linkages in sharing scarce facilities. There exists in African countries a network of research institutes and higher institutions of learning which needs to be developed.

RE-STRUCTURING THE EDUCATIONAL SYSTEM AND MANAGEMENT OF INSTITUTIONS

It might be useful to take the example of more developed countries where rapidly changing science and technology have forced major structural re-adjustments and re-training. Such structural adjustments are no doubt due to the competitive market situation. Throughout the developed countries, major structural changes leading to new approaches to educational planning have occured. This would seem the way to deal with the priority question and a situation which has saddled African countries with large pools of unemployable youths. Such an approach will enable the African region with scarce resources to significantly increase the output of trained scientific and technological manpower.

The third problem area in higher education in Africa concerns the management of higher education institutions both as a physical entity and as a community of scholars. Such institutions not only face the problem of lack of physical resources, but also of preserving a climate of human relations among scholars owing loyalty to the institutions and to the problems that beset national development.

Yet there are indications of serious management problems that are leading to brain-drain to other institutions. No amount of physical infrastructure can replace the essential need for vision among university staff and dedication to scholarship management. Persistent ethnicity and tribalism have not only been problems within the political leadership but also within the universities, which are wrongly considered as bases of power. The spatial distribution of higher institutions of learning and the staffing strength pose special problems that must be constantly but resolutely faced. The rush for promotional opportunities also tends to burden the institutions with inexperienced leadership.

The most important function of the universities is their role as a community of scholars interacting with policy makers and users of university-trained manpower in augmenting the accummulated knowledge.

Conclusion: The Critical Role of ICIPE

A great deal of thought has gone into the role of ICIPE since its inception. To those of us who have watched ICIPE grow, a number of important aspects stand out. The first is the vision of the founders and the dedication of staff to the objectives of the institution. ICIPE is a remarkable example of what men of good will can do in the cause of science.

Apart from its rationale as a centre of excellence, it is ICIPE's networking role that points to a possible solution to Africa's perpetual shortage of facilities and 'critical mass' of scientific and technological manpower.

However, the institution is among a number of research and training institutions both national and international. African countries must seriously address themselves to opportunities to share facilities and increase the area of collaboration within the limited resources the donor countries can afford. This will require a new international order in the advancement of science and technology.

POSTGRADUATE PROGRAMMES IN AFRICA: NEED FOR INNOVATIVE APPROACHES

J.S. Djangmah
Department of Zoology
University of Ghana
Legon, Ghana

Introduction

"The economic crisis affecting most of Africa has had a particularly damaging effect on higher education in the region. The universities, depending predominantly on government subventions, are faced with a situation in which the grants which governments are able to make available to them are dwindling in real terms from year to year while at the same time there are increasing and competing demands for the services of the institutions. In spite of this precarious situation which threatens the effectiveness of the impact of higher education institutions, the African people generally continue to regard higher education as a vital and critical element in the development effort of their countries".

These words aptly describe the circumstances of African universities as a whole. They came from the preface of the latest AAU publication: *Study on Cost Effectiveness and Efficiency in African Universities, May 1991.* Indeed, the excellent background paper prepared by ICIPE adequately covers the policy context within which this conference is being held but a few more statements are still relevant to my address and with your permission will be repeated.

"Research and postgraduate education: Expansion of Africa's capacity to produce its own intellectual talent to fill the highest scientific and technical jobs in educational establishments, in government and in the private sector is a critical matter to be addressed in building Africa's future..."

This statement is from the famous *World Bank Policy Study of Education in Sub-Sahara Africa, Jan., 1988.* These words echo dramatically sentiments expressed in the 1980 Lagos Plan of Action adopted by African Heads of State and Governments. It reflects the concerns of many African governments stretching back many years before the Lagos meeting.

The AAU and the United Nations Economic Commission for Africa (ECA) have addressed the roles of universities in meeting the challenge of indigenous capacity and capability building, particularly in scientific research and technology. In 1985, the AAU/ECA issued the *Mbabane Programme of Action: The Responses of the African Institutions of Higher Learning to Africa's Rapidly Deteriorating Economic and Social Conditions*. This was followed in 1987 by the *Harare Statement on Role of African Institutions of Higher Learning in Africa's Recovery and Development*.

Of particular interest to us today are two recent publications of the AAU. The first is the *Report on Graduate Education and R & D in African Universities* which came out in May 1990. The second is the report on Cost Effectiveness already mentioned. Both reports recommend measures to improve and expand postgraduate education in Africa, in the face of the inadequate staff, equipment and library resources of many of the universities. The rest of this paper will address some of these measures.

Local Postgraduate Schemes

"...Africa need not be consistently in the forefront of all scientific and technological advance, and well into the next century a sizeable fraction of Africa's Ph.D.s will still undoubtedly be trained in foreign institutions. But the continent nevertheless already needs to increase its capacity to absorb and use new knowledge, and that capacity is in large measure developed through indigenous postgraduate teaching and research programs."

This statement comes from the same World Bank Policy Study. The African universities themselves should be keenly aware that Africa should continue to tap the capacities and capabilities of the great centres of learning that exist outside the continent in the developed countries of Europe and America and also Asia. However the bulk of the training has to be done in Africa through new schemes that reflect the conditions to be found in our individual universities. Perhaps all would agree that graduate students in African institutions of higher learning can contribute through their research, solutions to local problems that may find immediate or long-term application. In many areas such as agriculture, food science, biology, public health, etc., the problems of Africa are waiting to be solved while some of the most talented young Africans are busily contributing more knowledge in areas remote to the continent's problems.

Joint Graduate Programme

The two AAU reports lamented the low enrolment in many of the postgraduate programmes and also noted the limited cooperation and linkages between African universities. The report on Cost Effectiveness and Efficiency recommended more regional cooperation and linkages:

> "Regional cooperation and linkages: Leadership of African universities should explore the possibility of greater regional cooperation and linkages in the implementation of their academic programmes. It is also recommended that the regional graduate school with international faculty drawn from individual university departments is adopted for major disciplines. The AAU should facilitate the process."

The Report on Graduate Education also favoured "the identification and selection of certain departments as centres for postgraduate training in particular disciplines". The World Bank study also agrees but warns that:

> "...Determining which institutions will participate in postgraduate programs of excellence will not be easy — for African governments or for their international partners. Questions of international and regional comparative advantage must be squarely faced, since resources will never be sufficient for every country in Africa or even for the continent as a whole to develop capacity at the highest level in all fields and sub-fields. Ultimately, decisions must be made discipline-by-discipline and in the light of regional requirements."

On the basis of the following criteria, certain departments were mentioned by the Report. These criteria are:

- existence of on-going graduate programmes
- staff strength
- quality of staff (ratio of professors to senior lecturers to lecturers)
- specialisation of staff
- laboratory equipment.

A meeting of deans of graduate education from ten selected universities from the West and Central African Region, held at Ibadan in May 1990 to deliberate the report, adopted this recommendation in the following words:

> "Considering the present difficult economic situation which limits the financial resources available to the continent, it is recommended that every effort should be made to identify institutions that are known to be good in certain disciplines and strengthen them in those disciplines".

Rectors, vice-chancellors and presidents of universities in West Africa, later that month met in Zaria, Nigeria. Among their recommendations are the following:

- Universities in the sub-region should collaborate in research.
- University researchers and teachers should have a working knowledge of English and French to facilitate mobility and understanding among them.
- Exchange of students, and professors, should be facilitated through a scheme supported by sponsors supportive of the idea.
- Centres of excellence should be created where special facilities exist.
- Planning and implementation of strategies for integration should be pursued with greater vigour than in the past.

All the actors and players agree on the actions that need to be taken. ICIPE has already taken the initiative by establishing the ARPPIS Ph.D. programme and also the sub-regional centres for the ARPPIS M.Sc. The present initiative to develop a **Graduate School** based at ICIPE is a logical step along the same road. The Director and management of ICIPE are to be congratulated for their foresight.

The AAU with the support of the donor community can take the initiative to look at other disciplines.

Research and Facilities Sharing

Well-maintained sophisticated equipment is not easy to come by in our universities. Scarcity of qualified technicians, the under-developed maintenance culture and the inadequacy of non-salary recurrent vote are to blame.

The Report on Graduate Education recommended a **Research Facilities Sharing Project** "to make it possible for the members of the Association of African Universities to share the use of selected specialised research equipment and facilities. Both staff and graduate students should go to where these facilities exist and use them for a specific period of time". Again, this is an accepted and common practice in the academic world. But with so many international boundaries and language barriers to cross, a funded project is required to ease the many burdens. Further action in this matter squarely rests with the AAU.

Joint Research Project's Programme

It was also suggested that inter-disciplinary research groupings could be assembled to tackle problems that can be said to be of interest to many African countries. Some suggested topics listed are:

- Effect of structural adjustment programmes on vulnerable groups in West and Central Africa.
- Socio-cultural background for the receptivity to scientific and technological innovative approaches to rural development catalysts among the different rural communities in West and Central Africa.
- Evaluation of local raw materials for various industrial uses and biotechnology.
- Semi-conductors synthesis: application to solar energy.
- Maternal, infant and child mortality in West and Central Africa.
- Trypanosomiasis and other animal diseases and animal management.
- Agroforestry.

Here again, with adequate funding and collaboration, such programmes would help achieve the critical mass of researchers to make them meaningful.

Research and Training Networks

The concept of the research network which links researchers located in different countries but who receive funding and the mutual stimulation at periodic meetings needs to be seriously studied and modified to suit African conditions. The African Economics Research Consortium (AERC) provides an effective model which can be adopted for other disciplines.

The AAU researchers recommended three networks initially based on:

- Medicinal plant research.
- Crop-processing, drying and storage.
- Small-scale irrigation; wetlands, and valley bottom-lands development.

The impact of the AERC arrangement on the research output, equipment acquisition and the morale of young economists in my university is remarkable. The staff involved have, through the projects they are participating in, acquired computers, photocopiers, etc. They have many travel opportunities and, more significantly, they are in more regular contact with their peers in other African countries.

Few African universities have the resources to provide this kind of material and intellectual support which alone can develop young faculty into experts. The ARPPIS Ph.D. programme and ARPPIS Sub-regional Centres for training of insect scientists at the M.Sc. level provides another concrete model for adoption in other disciplines.

The West African Health Community established by the Anglophone countries of ECOWAS, supports postgraduate medical education through a West African postgraduate medical college comprising the West African College of Surgeons and the West African College of Physicians.

The Carnegie Corporation of New York is currently funding collaborative postgraduate training in obstetrics and gynaecology by the two medical schools in Ghana, which are only 250 km apart. Some American medical schools – the University of Michigan, Ann Arbor and Johns Hopkins – are participating. Accra and Lome are even closer.

We should also welcome the African Capacity Building Foundation (ACB Foundation) recently launched by the World Bank and based in Harare, Zimbabwe.

Informatics, Information and Documentation

A 1990 report on *Assessment of Research in Basic Sciences and Technology in Africa*, issued by UNESCO/ROSTA, proposed the establishment of Documentation Centres and Specialised Data Banks in Africa so as to facilitate accessibility and dissemination of S & T information. No doubt various schemes are in operation to address this problem. It is crucial that these facilities are developed soon where appropriate.

Computers are fast coming to Africa and they are indeed necessary tools to encourage, yet the revolution in computer use in Africa is not being accompanied by training in materials science and micro-electronics. The scarcity of highly trained staff for teaching in computer science is seriously constraining many of our young fledgling departments. Again, sponsorship of regional training appears to be the only rational solution.

UNESCO/UNDP/ECA have already made a start with the African Institute of Informatics (AII). Unfortunately, we don't know much about this institute to be able to evaluate its impact.

What About Research Institutions and Centres of Excellence?

Before independence from colonial rule, Ghana and Nigeria shared the resources of the West African Cocoa Research Institute and the West African Oil Palm Research Institute. The new nationalism which later set in led to their break up. These major centres concentrated equipment, facilities and expertise in research on particular problems. Fortunately we can still count on the continent a number of such centres of excellence, i.e., ICIPE, ITTA, the International Livestock Centre for Africa (ILCA), etc. These centres of excellence have already achieved the critical masses of equipment and staff, both residents and visiting, to provide the enriched environments young researchers need to achieve, while their feet remain deeply rooted in the African soil and enmeshed in the solution of African problems. While all such centres can serve as the Woods Hole, Plymouth and CERN, for African scholars, their capacities to do more postgraduate training needs to be explored. ICIPE has demonstrated through the ARPPIS programme the capacity of the centres of excellence for postgraduate training. The postgraduate programme of the type envisaged by ICIPE is not only welcome to set standards of excellence for the universities and the other regional postgraduate centres mentioned above, but we can see the core of well-selected and motivated young research students enhancing the strategic research objectives of ICIPE.

It should naturally be the wish and hope of the AAU and well-meaning Africans and friends of Africa that the new but complementary roles of the centres of excellence benefit our universities as a whole.

Finally, we would wish to thank the Rockefeller Foundation for sponsoring this conference. We would also wish to thank the Director of ICIPE, Professor Thomas Odhiambo for involving the AAU in this worthy exercise. On behalf of the Secretary General of the AAU, on whose behalf I am here, I would wish to thank at this forum the many donor agencies whose concern for African development has been manifested in the numerous AAU projects they are supporting.

INSTITUTO VENEZOLANO DE INVESTIGACIONES CIENTÍFICAS (IVIC)

H.H. Vanegas
Director, IVIC
Caracas, Venezuela

Introduction

The Venezuelan Institute for Scientific Research (IVIC) was founded in February 1959 under the auspices of the Health Ministry (MSAS) in Altos de Pipe, halfway between Caracas and Los Teques.

This "science city" is located within 832 hectares of woods in a mild mountain climate at an altitude of 1,672m above sea level. These pleasant natural surroundings provide an ideal atmosphere for scientific research, and a backdrop to display the most important collection of Venezuelan outdoor sculpture in the country.

The scientific community consists of 104 professors, 131 visiting professors from universities throughout the world, 173 research associates, 59 research assistants, 182 students (49 undergraduates and 133 postgraduates), 314 administrative staff and 300 workers. A total of 58 laboratories are located within the various centers and departments. Thirty per cent of all international scientific publications produced every year in Venezuela originate from IVIC.

IVIC provided the launching point for the Venezuelan Petroleum Technological Institute (INTEVEP), the Engineering Institute (FII) and the International Institute for Advanced Studies (IDEA).

IVIC carries out three closely related types of activity:

- Basic and applied research.
- Graduate level teaching and technical training, coordinated by the Center for Advanced Studies.
- The provision of services and development of technology for other institutions and professionals, organised through the Center for Technology.

Centers and Departments

CENTER FOR BIOPHYSICS AND BIOCHEMISTRY

This Center conducts 62 projects in its 12 laboratories and coordinates postgraduate studies in the areas of biochemistry, physiology and biophysics, as well as training numerous under-graduates from universities working on their thesis projects.

The research interests of the Center lie in the following areas: structure of macromolecules and membranes, transport and deposition of cholesterol on arterial walls, blood-platelet aggregation mechanisms, energy flow and ionic transport in secretory and excretory epithelial tissues in terrestrial and aquatic organisms, ionic transport in nerves and muscles, excitation and contraction of muscles, action of neurotoxins and neurotransmitters, biochemistry and physiology of synaptic transmission, visual systems, physiological pain control, and digital processing of medical and dental images.

The Center possesses workshops for electronics and micromechanics, and offers services of microscopy, care and transportation of live specimens, crystallographic analysis of renal and bile stones, lipoprotein and cholesterol analysis, medical image processing, determination of L-carnitine amino acid in plasma and muscle tissues, and diagnostic tests for the susceptibility to malignant hyperthermia syndrome in humans.

CENTER FOR ECOLOGY AND ENVIRONMENTAL SCIENCES

The Center's five laboratories are currently undertaking 24 research projects and are involved in the coordination of postgraduate studies in the area of ecology. Researchers, technicians and students work together on applied and theoretical projects of great interest for Venezuela, both presently and in the future, covering various ecosystems such as forests, savannahs, agro-ecosystems, rivers, estuaries, and lakes. Palaeoecological studies re-create the environment in the geological past. Furthermore, research in ecosystems suffering the effects of urban and industrial activities (such as the Orinoco Oil Belt and the north-central coastal region) or natural disasters (such as earthquakes) are carried out.

CENTER FOR PHYSICS

The scientific and technological activities of this Center are carried out in seven laboratories and three specialised services. In general, the 43 research projects cover a wide range of topics: theoretical and solid-state physics, semiconductors, electromagnetism, quantum optics, magnetic resonance and superconductors, as well as molecular, atomic, nuclear and elementary particle physics. The Center also coordinates postgraduate studies in the area of physics.

NUCLEAR ENGINEERING SERVICE

The Nuclear Engineering Service provides technical assistance in matters related to the use of the RV-1 nuclear reactor and the Cobalt-60 source for scientific and technological purposes. The 3 megawatt RV-1 is the first and only nuclear reactor in Venezuela. IVIC is able to provide services in personnel training, production of radioactive isotopes of short half-life for industry, neutron activation analysis, neutrographs, and studies in neutron diffraction.

Through the use of the Cobalt-60 source, IVIC offers sterilisation services for medical and surgical material and radurisation (reduction of microbe populations) services for pharmaceutical products and for the support medium of the fertilizer Nitrobac. The source is also used in a project on food preservation through irradiation.

RADIOPHYSICS HEALTH SERVICE

This service provides radiological protection for the Institute and lends its expertise to many other institutions, as well as public and private companies which require radiological dosage recommendations and training in radiological protection procedures.

The laboratory for dosimetric calibration under the direction of the Radiophysics Health Service, is projected to become the first national center for the calibration of doses used in radiotherapy, for the calibration and control of radiotherapy and radiodiagnosis equipment, and for radiological protection, as well as for the elaboration of dosage calibration curves.

CRYOGENIC SERVICE

This service is in charge of liquefying and distributing helium and nitrogen for the laboratories at IVIC.

CENTER FOR EXPERIMENTAL MEDICINE

A total of five laboratories undertake 28 applied and theoretical research projects with priority in health problem areas of the country. The Center trains medical and paramedical specialists and coordinates postgraduate studies in the areas of immunology, human genetics, and biochemistry. Information is actively exchanged with other institutions within the country and abroad, and its laboratories are international reference centers for iron deficiency, histocompatibility antigens, abnormal fibrinogens, and the standardisation of thromboplastins. Furthermore, the Center offers out-patient services for genetic diseases.

CENTER FOR MICROBIOLOGY AND CELL BIOLOGY

The Center's eight laboratories undertake research on 30 projects in the following areas: environmental allergens, molecular biology and epidemiology of viral diarrhea in humans and pigs, cellular biology of cancer, immunology of schistosomiasis, malaria, leishmaniasis and Chagas' disease, virulence mechanisms of encephalitis equina and AIDS, plant viruses in cash crops, biological fertilizers for legumes based on *Rhizobium*, physiological dimorphism of zoopathogenic fungi, and the application of micro-organisms in oil extraction. Besides these projects, the Center is developing several biotechnological programs for the diagnosis of viral hepatitis, auto-immune diseases, schistosomiasis and malaria.

The Center also coordinates postgraduate studies in the area of microbiology and collaborates on the programs in the areas of biochemistry and immunology. Furthermore, an epidemiological warning service is offered for encephalitis equina, dengue, yellow fever and other arboviruses.

CENTER FOR CHEMISTRY

The Center includes ten laboratories dealing with 51 research projects in many different areas including development of new analytical methods to measure traces of heavy metals in biological fluids, atmosphere and food stuffs; chemical characterisation of the atmosphere and the biogenic emissions released into the air; catalysts for petrochemical processes; transition metal complexes; kinetics and mechanisms of organic reactions; synthesis and characterisation of organic compounds, etc.

The Center coordinates postgraduate studies in the area of chemistry, provides many services for industry, and maintains an instrumental analysis service to characterise chemical products and materials.

ANTHROPOLOGY DEPARTMENT

The Department is organised into four laboratories which carry out special research projects in both theoretical and applied anthropology. The Department also has an educational purpose, offering the Magister and doctoral degrees, which are the only graduate degree programs in anthropology in Venezuela.

The guiding orientation of the department's 14 research projects is to contribute to the understanding of socio-cultural patterns and processes among the ethnically and culturally diverse human populations of Venezuela. These projects include studies in archaeology, ethnohistory, contemporary ethnic peoples, peasant populations, processes of urbanisation, and rural-urban migration. Applied research is geared toward the preservation of cultural resources and the design and implementation of regional economic and social development programs.

DEPARTMENT OF SCIENCE STUDIES

The main activities of the Department are research on the sociology and the history of science in Venezuela and in Latin America, and postgraduate teaching.

Relating the history of Venezuelan science, the research focuses on the process of institutionalisation, specifically on the foundation and development of institutions both past and present. In the area of sociology of science, research deals with the views, interests and strategies of scientists, the questions related to the functioning of scientific communities in the specific context of Latin America, and the images of scientific and technical processes held by different sectors of the Venezuelan society. Throughout, there is an interest on the comparative perspective with other Latin American countries.

The Department owns a collection of 3,000 volumes on sociology, history, politics and philosophy of science in the "Olga Gasparini" library which is open to students and researchers from within and outside IVIC.

DEPARTMENT OF MATERIALS SCIENCE

The Department's three laboratories conduct nine research projects in the following areas: physico-chemical treatments of minerals and synthetic materials, investigated through X-ray diffraction, infrared spectroscopy, differential thermal analysis and electron microscopy; geochemical analysis of sediments using X-ray fluorescence to identify a wide range of elements (including the transition series), as well as other analytical techniques for biological materials; and finally, magnetic ceramics, semiconducting ternary and other types of alloys, and the densification of alumina.

MATHEMATICS DEPARTMENT

The Laboratory of Mathematical Analysis is the only laboratory of the Institute's Mathematics Department. Postgraduate teaching and research are carried out in the following areas: algebra, functional analysis, partial differentiation equations, mathematical logic and foundations of set theory, theory of functions and probability theory.

International Centers at IVIC

CENTER FOR BIOLOGICAL SCIENCES (CLAB)

CLAB is a center created by agreement between UNESCO and the Venezuelan Government to promote the teaching of biological sciences and to foster integration and cooperation in this discipline throughout Latin America and the Caribbean region. The Center has organised 22 high-level international courses for Latin American students to date.

The Bioscience Information Network for Latin America and the Caribbean is a project within CLAB and under the auspices of the General Information Progam of UNESCO. It aims to produce a data bank for the biosciences and their applications for Latin America and the Caribbean. It will provide relevant information on research projects, researchers, institutions, courses and equipment, for scientists, educators and government officials in the areas of science, technology and industry.

INTERNATIONAL CENTER FOR TROPICAL ECOLOGY

This Center was established through an agreement between UNESCO and IVIC in order to facilitate and promote both research and teaching in tropical ecology, as well as to stimulate the cooperation in the tropical region through the interchange of scientists and the organisation of international courses, meetings and seminars.

The Center has been working in close collaboration with the Man and the Biosphere Program, especially in the MAB projects related to savannas of the Orinoco Llanos, Amazonian rain forest and paramos of the Venezuelan Andes.

The activities of the International Centers are summarised below:

- *Centro Latinoamericano de Ciencias Biologicas (CLAB) of UNESCO*
  21 2-week courses at graduate and post-doctoral level
  600 attending students from Latin America and Caribbean
  300 lecturers worldwide

- *Biosciences Information Network for Latin America and the Caribbean*
  Operates a data bank on biology, biotechnology and biomedicine in L.A.C. under the auspices of UNESCO's General Information Program

- *Centro Internacional de Ecologia Tropical (CIET) of UNESCO*
  14 international and 40 national meetings conducted
  Man and the Biosphere (MAB) program of UNESCO

In addition, numerous agreements exist for academic exchange and cooperation with institutions and academics worldwide. In 1990, there were 91 international visiting scientists at IVIC.

Center for Technology

RESEARCH, DEVELOPMENT AND CONSULTANCY SERVICES

This Center provides technological assistance to tackle problems of national development. The Center organises multi-disciplinary research projects, develops new products and technical processes, and offers technical assistance to government, ministries, hospitals, private companies and individuals in Venezuela and the Caribbean.

The Center thus channels requests for research projects and analytical services in the following areas: analytical chemistry, petrochemistry, natural products, environmental pollution, nuclear engineering, low temperature and liquification techniques, medicine, agriculture, precision mechanics, quality control of chemical products, and inspection of radioactive sources. The Center also supervises the production and sale of the NITROBAC fertilizer, the diamond knife and diagnostic medical kits.

DIAMOND KNIFE WORKSHOP

The diamond knife is an essential tool used in electron microscopy to produce extremely thin tissue preparations. Besides manufacturing the diamond knife, the workshop produces specialist opthalmic scalpels for precision cornea operations.

DIVISION FOR THE MAINTENANCE, DESIGN AND CONSTRUCTION OF SCIENTIFIC EQUIPMENT

In workshops fitted out with precision mechanics, electronic and refrigeration machinery, the Division designs, constructs and repairs much of the equipment used in the Institute's laboratories.

Quimbiotec C.A.

IVIC and the Venezuelan Investment Fund created the QUIMBIOTEC company with the objective of constructing and operating a blood plasma fractionation plant to produce, on an industral scale, blood derivatives such as albumin, gamma globulins and human anti-haemophilic factors. The facilities are presently in the final phase of construction. The plant is designed to process up to 40,000 litres of human blood plasma annually and is projected to cover the nation's requirements and eventually those of the Andean Region. Furthermore, QUIMBIOTEC will also sell diagnostic medical kits, medicines, fertilizers and other chemical and biological products.

"Marcel Roche" Library

With a collection of 60,000 books and subscriptions to more than 4,000 technical and scientific journals, the library at IVIC is the most important in Latin America in the fields of science and technology. Every year the library offers its services to some 60,000 researchers, teachers, students, doctors, engineers and other professionals from within IVIC and from all parts of Venezuela. The library also offers a photocopying service (over a million copies yearly) for users who can request copies personally or by fax, telex, telephone or letter. The library is open from Mondays to Fridays between 8:30 am and 9:30 pm, and on weekends from 8:30 am to 4:30 pm. At present a new modern building is under construction.

The library is presently undergoing a major automatisation process which will provide an efficient computerised service directly linked to national and international data bases. The system will be linked to the Public Data Transmission Network of the state telephone company (CANTY), to the National Library and other scientific libraries in the country, and to the Automated Science and Technology System (SAICYT) at the nation's Science and Technology Council (CONICIT). This technical updating of the library facilities will create a regional center worthy of UNESCO's designation as the "Center for Scientific and Technological Documentation and Information for Latin America and the Caribbean".

Computer Network

The computer network for scientific and administrative purposes presently being installed, will consist of 11 main workstations and servers located in the research centers and departments, the administrative building and the library, each with several associated computers, and all connected by fiber optics.

Scientific and Technical Cooperation Agreements

IVIC has established cooperation agreements with many scientific and technological institutions throughout the world. These agreements further international collaboration on research projects, provide basic and specialist training of personnel and promote the sharing of experiences through the interchange of professionals.

At the moment IVIC has 22 agreements with national institutions including the Central University (UCV), the Simon Bolivar University (USB), the University of the Eastern Region (UDO) and the Venezuelan Petroleum Technological Institute (INTEVEP), and 17 agreements with foreign institutions in the USA, Israel, the Soviet Union, Spain, Colombia, and others.

Prizes and Awards

Scientists at IVIC have repeatedly received prizes and awards in recognition of their work. Fourteen researchers have won the "Lorenzo Mendoza Fleury" Prize awarded by the Polar Foundation for the most outstanding scientists in Venezuela. IVIC scientists have also been awarded the CONICIT Annual Prize such as the National Award for Science, and for the Best Scientific Paper, The Central University's "Francisco De Venanzi" Prize and the IBM award for Science and Technology. At the international level, IVIC scientists have received the "Manuel Noriega Morales" Award from the Organisation of American States, the John Simon Guggenheim Foundation Award and UNESCO's "Kalinga" Award.

Art and Science

Scientific research is one of the highest aspirations of mankind, as is the aesthetic appreciation of art. IVIC provides an ideal atmosphere for both in its open spaces graced with sculpture and paintings by many of Venezuela's leading artists.

Center for Advanced Studies

The educational activities of IVIC are planned and coordinated by the Center for Advanced Studies with the collaboration of all the research centers and departments of the Institute. The Center promotes the training of scientific personnel in three different ways:

- The Institute's graduate students can participate in M.Sc. and Ph.D. programmes in the areas of physics, chemistry, mathematics, and biology with majors in immunology, human genetics, physiology and biophysics, biochemistry, ecology, and anthropology. Also, university students can take subjects in any of these areas to further their studies.

- Visiting researchers, technicians and students at university or postgraduate level can obtain professional research experience in any of the Institute's laboratories directly under the supervision of a researcher, or receive training in the use of equipment, and in new techniques and methodologies. Students from other institutions are welcome to benefit from IVIC's facilities to conduct their research.

- Short specialised courses on the latest developments at the forefront of scientific knowledge are also offered for young scientists from all parts of the world. Local and international experts are frequently invited to participate as teachers. The Center has coordinated the teaching of more than 500 Ph.D. and M.Sc. students, 938 undergraduate fellows, 283 undergraduate students on special research projects, as well as 333 students for course credit and 281 professionals-in-training. Teaching is conducted through lectures and through direct guidance, which is tailored to the individual student's needs and creates an atmosphere that fosters a productive interchange of ideas between students and researchers.

A summary of the organisation and programmes of the Graduate School (CEA) is shown in Tables 1 and 2, and Table 3 lists other research institutes in Latin America which operate postgraduate programmes.

Future Plans and Projects

IVIC aims to continue the scientific and technological research projects presently being undertaken, as well as to open up new areas of research, to maintain its high level of postgraduate programs and to provide technical assistance to other institutions and professionals. Of prime importance for the next five years is the incorporation of 50 young scientists whose vitality and leadership will take on the important role of contributing to the nation's development.

TABLE 1: THE ACADEMIC PROGRAM OF THE CENTRO DE ESTUDIOS AVANZADOS (CEA) GRADUATE SCHOOL

Postgraduate Programs

Leading to Magister Scientiarum degree

    24 course credit units + 6 credits required for thesis = 30 credits

    1 foreign language (English)

    2 years of study

    Supported by full fellowships (living expenses + tuition)

Table 1 Contd...

Table 1, Contd.

Leading to Philosphus Scientiarum (doctoral) degree
    45 course credit units + 15 credits for thesis = 60 credits
    2 foreign languages (English + other)
    4 years including M.Sc. or 3 years straight
    Supported by full fellowships (living expenses + tuition)

Pre-graduate Programs
    For students registered at universities
    No formal courses
    Technical training, theoretical tutoring and feasible research
    Supported by partial fellowships

Extension Programs
    Thesis research by graduate students registered at universities
    Short high-level international courses, e.g., CLAB, CIET, ICTP, ICC, EC
    (supported by fellowships)

Student Enrolment Per Year (1986-90)

Program	Applicants Admitted	Enrolled	Graduating
Master's	46%	80	32
Doctoral (Ph.Sc.)	39%	19	5
Pre-graduate	70%	68	-

Table 1, Contd.

Table 1, Contd.

Total number of graduating students (1973-91)

Master's degree	454
Doctoral (Ph.Sc.) degree	67
Total	521

Location of professionals (M.Sc. and Ph.Sc.) graduated from IVIC

Universities and higher learning institutions in Venezuela	250
Abroad	44
Public industry and business	20
Private industry and business	15
Unknown	192
Total	521

TABLE 2: ADMINISTRATION OF THE IVIC GRADUATE SCHOOL (CEA)

CEA Commission
    Appointed by IVIC's Director for a 2-year term
    Dean (reports to IVIC's Director and Directive Council)
    Vice-Dean
    3 Principal Members
    3 Deputy Members

Area Coordinators (report to the Dean)

    Biology: one coordinator each in Biochemistry, Physiology and Biophysics, Immunology, Human Genetics, Ecology, Microbiology, Anthropology.
    Chemistry
    Mathematics
    Physics

Staff (18)
    Coordinator, Assistant Coordinator, 3 Physiologists, English Teacher, 2 Information and Audiovisual Assistants, Administrator, 2 Administrative Assistants, 3 Secretaries, 2 Filing Clerks, Telephone Operator, Cleaner

1991 Budget (US$)

Personnel (staff)	85,000
Supplies (office)	16,000
Equipment (office)	2,000
Teaching Programs*	143,000
Total	246,000

  * Includes faculty fees and honorariums, some student fellowships, aid for thesis research, student travel for field work and scientific meetings, etc.

Fellowships (US$ per year)

Living expenses	6,000 (for Graduate Student in Venezuela)
Tuition	820 (for IVIC)

TABLE 3: OTHER LATIN AMERICAN RESEARCH INSTITUTIONS OFFERING POSTGRADUATE PROGRAMS

MEXICO

Centro de Investigación y Docencia Económica

>Mathematics applied to economics, political sciences, Latin American studies. Economics, international politics.

Instituto Nacional de Investigaciones sobre Recursos Bióticos

>Ecology and biotic resources.

Centro de Investigación Científica y de Educación Superior de Ensenada

>Physical optics, high resonance devices and circuits, electronic instrumentation, geophysical instrumentation, telecommunications, larval ecology of marine fish, plankton ecology, benthonic ecology, marine pollution, coastal lagoon dynamics, seismotectonics, computational seismology, geophysics.

Centro Panamericano de Estudios e Investigaciones Geográficas

>Applied geography

Colegio de Mexico

>Latin American studies, anthropology, archeology, economics, politics.

Centro de Investigación y Estudios Avanzados del Instituto Politécnico

>Cell biology, biochemistry, biotechnology and bioengineering, pharmacology, toxicology, physiology and biophysics, neurosciences, genetics, chemistry, education, physics, electronic engineering, mathematics, educational mathematics.

BRAZIL

Instituto de Matemática Pura e Aplicada

>M.Sc. and Ph.D. in mathematics.

Instituto de Física Pura e Aplicada

>M.Sc. and Ph.D. in physics.

ROLE OF RESEARCH CENTRES IN POSTGRADUATE TRAINING IN INDIA

Y.P. Singh
Indian Agricultural Research Institute (IARI)
New Delhi, India

Introduction

India is primarily an agricultural country. Nearly 80% of its population directly or indirectly depends for its livelihood on agriculture. The position remains stationary and will continue to be so despite rapid industrialisation. Since its independence in 1947, the country has been laying great emphasis on agricultural development and has achieved great success on this front. A major infrastructure development has been the creation of a chain of institutions for agricultural education and research. Fortunately, the country inherited a number of agricultural colleges, research centres and a nucleus of teacher-scientists from British India. These two assets, backed by external help, greatly facilitated the creation and development of its network of agricultural universities and research centres across the length and breadth of the country. These institutions have played a significant role in the process of modernising Indian agriculture. Their role is the creation, conservation and communication of knowledge. The agricultural universities perform all three of these roles. The research centres perform a double research and extension role and simultaneously provide support to education.

The role of research centres in postgraduate education when looked at in retrospect can be grouped under three headings:

- role enlargement
- role assimilation and
- role support.

Role Enlargement

Role enlargement refers to role expansion in covering postgraduate training. The best example of this is provided by the Indian Agricultural Research Institute, the National Dairy Research Institute and the Indian Veterinary Research Institute (IARI). The case of the Indian Agricultural Research Institute, in particular, is noteworthy because it has provided leadership and manpower for building agricultural universities and research centres in the country.

THE IARI POST-GRADUATE SCHOOL

The IARI was established in the year 1905 with a donation by Phipps of the USA. Its primary role was to conduct research in different facets of agriculture. It used to offer a post-graduate diploma in agricultural science, mainly for the in-service candidates. Soon after independence, with the catalytic action of the Rockefeller Foundation, it planned to set up a post-graduate school to offer M.Sc. and Ph.D. programmes to fulfil the requirements for highly qualified manpower that would be needed for agricultural development. Later, the Government of India granted it the status of a deemed university. Rockefeller Foundation provided material and non-material support.

The setting up of a Post-graduate School at IARI was a significant breakthrough for the following reasons. An established institution with an existing leadership status, it underwent role transformation to cope with the future demand that was to fall on the country. It adopted changes without any major budgetary or structural implications. The administrative structure remained the same. Only a limited number of posts were added requiring only a minor hike in the budget. It was built upon what the institute had, rather than starting from scratch. It is noteworthy that reconstruction is more complex than construction, but the case of IARI provides an example of successful reconstruction.

Not only was a new programme added, but it was also based on a new system of education. The P.G. School was an institution with a difference. It was based on course credits under the trimester system. Hitherto, the Indian institutions were based on a system of annual examination with external examiners, which the Radhakrishnan Committee called the "greatest ill" of the Indian educational system. Today, all agricultural universities and a host of other prestigious institutions follow this system, but the Post-graduate School of IARI was the first to adopt it and adapt it to Indian conditions.

The entire job of transformation was executed by Indians in India under the leadership of Ralph Cummings who also acted as the first Dean, but handed over this role to Dr. A.B. Joshi soon after. At no stage did the campus appear American-dominated, nor did it have many Americans present.

The experience of IARI served as a guide to other agricultural universities which came up in the following years. The staff, equipment, farmers, laboratories and the precious library of the original IARI (i.e. the institute without the P.G. School) was of great help to the post-graduate students who themselves became a great help in expanding the frontiers of knowledge. This new manpower which entered the institute had unique attributes. Being young, they were more energetic, highly motivated, able to work under a deadline with additional vigour, and bright and creative.

The selection procedure was designed to trap the most capable student from any part of the large country that India is. The P.G. School was based on the following cardinal principles:

- select the best,
- give them the best,
- thoroughly test.

All these made the P.G. students more productive and over the years, they became the most valuable resources in the Institute.

From the point of view of pedagogy, the Post-graduate School is a case of one of the most distinguished educational innovations. Most educational innovations fail or create problems but here was a case of a bright success which has gone unrecorded in the literature of educational change. How did this change take place and who was the agent of change behind it? A systematic answer to this question would be a valuable contribution in the area of institution building. I have not done any study nor are such studies encouraged in agricultural settings. However as a distant observer of this process as a student, and later as alumnus, and subsequently as faculty of this great school, I can venture an impressionistic commentary.

Well, Ralph Cummings was the main change agent behind it. He, with the active cooperation of the Indian trio (Drs. B.P. Pal, A.B. Joshi and M.S. Swaminathan), initiated and carried on the mission. That the Institute recognises the contribution of Dr. Cummings is evident from the fact that it has named its biggest laboratory after him. The institute invited him for its most prestigous lecture – the Lal Bahadur Shastri Memorial Lecture – the only foreigner to have been invited for it.

Much later, the Indian Veterinary Research Institute and the National Dairy Research Institute, two of our major research institutes in the field of livestock, acquired a Post-graduate School. They did not have to struggle as much, as the IARI example and experience, as well as that of several agricultural universities, was available to them. They too have had a happy experience with their respective Post-graduate Schools.

Role Assimilation

An example of role assimilation is provided by the Sugarcane Research Institute at Pusa, in Bihar, which has been metamorphosed into the Rajendra Agricultural University. This institute had nearly 2,000 acres of land, housing, offices and a laboratory complex and was located in the main agricultural belt of Bihar. When the proposal for an agricultural university was mooted in the state, the expert committee selected this as the site for the university. The Government of Bihar transferred the Institute and all its assets to the University. Today, a full-fledged university has come up on this site and the Institute has become an organic part of it. The staff of the Institute have become the faculty. While sticking to the main charter of the Institute, the staff of the Institute participate in teaching. As a matter of fact, they are the integral part of the faculty. With the assistance of post-graduate students, the research of the Institute has conquered new frontiers while the students benefit through the expertise and facility of the Institute.

Role Support

Under this group are the research centres within or outside the control of universitites which have established a symbiotic or a supportive relationship. Under the symbiotic relationship are the forms in which both stand to gain from each other by collaboration. Many of the Indian Council of Agricultural Research (ICAR) institutes have signed a memorandum of understanding with agricultural universities. In this arrangement, students do the course work on the campus but carry out research in the institutes. In this way the institute gets the advantage of Doctoral and Masters students who, in turn, are benefitted by the expert guidance (by some of the top men in their respective fields), fellowship and facilities of the institute. We have this kind of collaboration with some international institutes also. Most popular in this type of collaboration is the IARI-IRRI collaboration. Several of the IARI students have conducted their research at the IRRI. Both stand to gain by this process. The sub-station staff of IARI are entitled for faculty membership.

In some cases where the research station staff do not get students, these research stations provide expertise on specific problems and on specific localities which is learnt by students through visits to these places or by special lectures by the staff of those centres.

Further Strengthening the Collaborative Relationships

There is still scope for further strengthening such collaborations. In my opinion the IARI and the other strong universities should enter into a memorandom of understanding with all the international institutes on the lines of that existing between IARI and IRRI. For this arrangement the international institutes have also to show willingness as a symbolic measure rather than as aid or assistance. Some fellowships may have to be instituted and working arrangements for joint guidance needs to be worked out. Back home there is plenty of scope to weld together the post-graduate programme with the research centres.

At this stage, India offers a picture of developmental differential. As a result of planned development, some areas have become highly developed, others moderately, while some miserably lag behind. Their own institutions are neither well-equipped nor well-staffed although the research centres have been established. A clear case in this regard is that of North-Eastern region, which has lagged behind in agricultural development but has tremendous potential. Although several research centres have come up, left on their own they will take time to deliver the goods. It is, therefore, important that the mother institutes like the IARI should take more interest in them. Because of the hazardous conditions prevailing in that region, people do not like to be posted there permanently, but are ready to contribute on a visiting and cooperative basis.

If somebody from the IARI base is asked to collaborate with the local staff, many more would come forward. Similarly, students can be encouraged to take up problems in these areas. Right now, one of my own students is working in that area and we have a happy experience with the problem and the product. However, this kind of venture requires a certain infrastructure, as well as budgetary support. Similarly, we should also encourage the development of voluntary groups comprising the staff of different institutions to work on some common important problems. These are only a few of the various possibilities which start emerging the moment we start thinking in terms of collaboration.

MULTI-DISCIPLINARY INSTITUTIONAL MODELS FOR GRADUATE TRAINING IN INSECT SCIENCE

O.A. Adeyeye
Department of Biological Sciences
Duquesne University
Pittsburgh, Pennsylvania

Introduction

Two weeks ago, I was not aware of the existence of any place called Bellagio. It was only ten days ago that I received a telephone call from Professor James Oliver Jr., and learned that he had nominated me to represent him at this conference. In all truthfulness, I did not take the nomination too seriously. For one thing, I felt that my feet were too tiny to step into the giant shoes of a towering person of the stature of Professor Oliver. For another, I was apprehensive that an African scientist who now resides in the USA would be considered as part of the chronic and acute brain drain problems that face not only Africa, but indeed, the entire so-called Third World. It was a pleasant surprise to receive the invitation to this meeting of truly distinguished minds. I must expess my sincere gratitude to Professor Odhiambo for the invitation to this august conference.

I brought with me the very best wishes of the immediate past president of the Entomological Society of America (ESA), Professor James H. Oliver Jr. As some of you know, Professor Oliver is also the Special Foreign Affairs Representative on the governing board of the ESA. He asked me to express his abiding interest in the theme of this conference and to wish us the most fruitful deliberations. As a close associate of Professor Oliver, I can testify to his desire to foster strong cooperation between the ESA and entomological associations in all parts of the world. It has been a privilege for me to represent Africa on the International Affairs Committee of the Entomological Society of America. However, I would not pretend to be representing the ESA at this meeting. Rather, I represent, even if unofficially, the present and future generation of *African* youth who stand to gain the most from the creation of a sustainable science leadership on our continent.

Without a doubt, generations to come would regard the 20th century as one of the greatest periods of scientific breakthroughs for the human race. So astounding is the rate of progress in scientific knowledge and technological advancement that doctoral dissertations which may be considered brilliant today have no guarantee that they will not be confined to shelves laden with dust and cobwebs by the year 2000. It is no secret that many scientific and technological innovations are reduced to mere obsolescence in the span of a decade. Biblical King Solomon was most apt to have written: "To the making of books, there is no end".

One indisputable trend in science has been the convergence towards a multi-disciplinary approach. Times were, when one might have argued that because of scarcity of resources, African scientists should devote their energy solely to the "applied sciences". Even in a country like the USA, with its abundance of resources, much attention is properly being focused on educational reform. Some of the questions occasionally raised both within and outside academe are: What is the proper balance between research and teaching at research-oriented universities; what are the benefits and costs associated with these dual roles; how does university-based research contribute to society? Given the limitations of resources, should research efforts be devoted exclusively to those areas of immediate practical applications? A few words might, therefore, be in order about the need to conduct research in the basic as well as applied insect sciences.

The Basic Sciences - Technology Link

Our very presence at this conference underscores our appreciation of the need for having a strong science/technology base to advance society's material well being. An article entitled "Science, Technology and the Western Miracle", by Rosenberg and Birdzell Jr., that appeared in the November 1990 edition of *Scientific American* provides an illuminating historical perspective. The Industrial Revolution, which began around 1800 and which has propelled the West to their present economic position, began a period of long-term economic growth that has made the West richer and more powerful than the rest of the world. Explanations for this "Western Miracle", according to Rosenberg and Birdzell, often have been deficient and inconsistent (in the light of numerous counter-examples), emphasising advantages related to colonialism and the presence of natural resources. They cite as a far more plausible explanation, however, the strong links that developed between the growth of scientific knowledge and the rise of technology — what we now refer to as technology transfer.

Initially, Western technology developed within the economic sphere, with science itself contributing little to economic growth despite major scientific discoveries dating back as far as Galileo and the Renaissance. But by the early 19th century, Western science had begun "a better organised attack on the secrets of nature and used greater resources in the assault than science in other cultures". Western science then organised itself into specific disciplines, and scientists were brought together in academic institutions equipped for directed research. Perhaps most important, as the authors pointed out, Western science adopted "a single standard of truth based on observation, reason, experiment and replicability", enabling both cross-fertilisation among the branch of sciences and the application of scientific discoveries to practical ends. Indeed, because of empirical methods which Western scientists adopted, they were required to engage in those real-world problems often dictated by the need for economic productivity.

Paul Christiano, former Dean of the Carnegie Institute of Technology, recently made a case for strong basic sciences as the essential cornerstone for technological pre-eminence[1]. Citing numerous examples of research centres at Carnegie Mellon University, where he is now the Academic Provost, Christiano pointed out the increasing reliance by industry on university-based research. He noted that these research centres are sufficiently diversified so as to provide decentralised decision-making mechanisms on the academic side that reflect analogous mechanisms in American business.

As we deliberate on a sustainable leadership for insect sciences in Africa, we must quickly reject the false dichotomy of scientific endeavours into the "basic sciences" on the one hand and the "applied sciences" on the other. The overwhelming evidence from the history of science is that the great advances in basic sciences have inexorably led to giant strides in scientific applications and technological innovations. Similarly, the so-called applied sciences have provided springboards for the explosion of theoretical and basic scientific principles. A few examples would suffice to drive home this point.

The ambitious human genome project, the world-wide efforts of genetic engineering of crop plants, the use of biotechnological methods to produce drugs such as insulin and the use of the polymerase chain reaction and DNA sequencing for molecular fingerprinting in solving crimes, are all predicated on the discovery of the molecular basis for heredity and the characterisation of the DNA molecule. These are classic examples of basic sciences providing powerful tools for practical applications to human needs. With regards to the application of molecular biology to solve practical human needs, the best is yet to come. This is the golden age for biological sciences. My own lab is presently engaged in a collaborative project with the Science and Technology Center of the Carnegie Mellon University in Pittsburgh to develop biotechnological assays for studying vector-host relationships in tick-borne diseases. If our efforts succeed, as I pray they will, we would be having potentially revolutionary tools for diagnosing some tick-borne diseases.

---

1 Christian, P.F. 1990. Why university-based research in engineering and science is essential. *CIT* (The magazine of the Carnegie Institute of Technology), **10** (1), 4-5.

While we applaud these obvious contributions of basic science to meeting practical needs, one must quickly point out that the genealogy of molecular biology includes people whose primary interest were practical human needs. Frederick Griffith, for instance, was primarily interested in developing a vaccine against *Streptococcus pneumoniae*. Yet by a gratuitous serendipity, he was the first to document the capacity of bacteria to incorporate external nucleic acid into their genome. Barbara McClintock's work on corn genetics led to the discovery of transposons. Today, the technique of bacterial transformation is one of the cornerstones of molecular biology and genetic engineering, while knowledge of transposable elements has elevated our understanding of molecular genetics to new heights. There are of course multitudes of other examples of the inextricability of basic and applied sciences.

Engaging solely in applied sciences is a luxury that Africa cannot afford. To do that would be intellectual suicide. Benjamin Mays, the great teacher and former President of Morehouse College, Atlanta, often said that, "In the race of life, the person behind must run faster than the person ahead or remain forever behind". I cannot conceive of a truly sustainable insect science leadership in Africa outside of a programme that combines sound foundations in basic sciences with rigorous efforts in applied entomology. Such programmes are already in existence in many universities across the USA, Western Europe, Japan and Israel.

The Multi-Disciplinary Approach to Insect Science Education

In the United States, the evolution of graduate entomology curricula has reflected the understanding that a multi-disciplinary approach is a *sine qua non* for modern sciences in general and, in particular, for a multi-faceted discipline like entomology. Thus, in addition to requirements for courses in traditional areas like insect taxonomy, toxicology, physiology, ecology, morphology, etc., many departments now have such courses as chemical ecology, insect endocrinology, modelling, etc. In addition, students are required to take a regime of courses outside their department. The regime of extra-departmental courses prescribed for a student by his or her advisory committee is often a reflection of the area of specialisation of the student. For example, a student specialising in chemical ecology may be required to take various classes in botany, ecology, and biochemistry, while another student specialising in insect toxicology or physiology is required to take classes in pharmacology, pharmacokinetics, biochemistry and biophysics. A student who specialises in integrated pest management may be required to take further classes in calculus, statistics, and computer science.

Needless to say, these regimes of classes are usually rigorous, but the benefits from such an eclectic training are immediately obvious: the production of scientists having enough depth to become specialists, as well as the necessary breadth to interact with others whose expertise would enhance one's success in a chosen entomological speciality. Of course, such a multiple course system takes time. All good ventures do. It is better to spend six extra months in graduate school than to produce half-baked doctorates who are not equipped to face the stupendous challenges of modern scientific enquiry. To be candid, one must say that even in the USA, many entomologists were slow to embrace the new frontiers of biological sciences. "DNA jockeying", is a derogatory reference to molecular biology, which some feel should be prevented from an aggressive metastasis that would endanger traditional entomology! In this regard, Professor Oliver, in one of his presidential messages this past year, challenged members of the ESA against a mental inertia that resists progress and change. Such a warning is most apt as we consider a sustainable insect science leadership in Africa.

With regards to models for such a multi-disciplinary postgraduate programme, it is obvious from the foregoing paragraphs that I strongly favour a course system akin to that operating in most U.S. graduate schools. All of us, for better or for worse, perceive the world from the windows of our prior experiences. I would concede my being handicapped by experiences that must be considered quite limited in comparison with those of most of you at this august conference. This notwithstanding, empirical and verifiable evidence suggests that, whereas one can question the quality of science education at the undergraduate level in the USA, at the graduate level, American science education is the best in the world. In any case, the suggestion is not that we embrace any model in absolute totality without regards to its applicability in the African context. Many U.S. schools are dropping the traditional requirement of a foreign language for the science doctoral students. The argument is that since as much as 70% of scientific information is available in English, acquisition of computer literacy (an electronic language) is more beneficial to scientific endeavours than competence in other languages. While we must ensure that all African scientists acquire computer literacy, the reality that English and French are the official languages for most of Africa would make it desirable that educated Africans acquire at least a reading knowledge in both languages. Only when we can communicate with each other can we engage in meaningful cooperative projects for the uplifting of Africa. As the blackfly migrates from Ghana to Togo, it pays little attention to the international boundary and the change in official language! Ghanaians and Togolese scientists had better be able to communicate with each other so that they can organise a concerted effort against this formidable vector of river blindness.

As many of you know, most of the entomology departments in the USA are located in the Land Grant universities. On the average, these universities are endowed with the kind of human, financial and infra-structural resources that African universities cannot even begin to imagine. I obtained my M.Sc. from the University of Florida, Gainesville. At that time, there were over one hundred graduate students in the department, with about eighty engaged in doctoral studies in entomology! The faculty consisted of 33 full-time faculty and another 54 adjunct faculty located in various federal and state laboratories throughout the state of Florida. In Gainesville, often referred to as the entomological capital of the world, there were about two hundred people with the Ph.D. in entomology or related sciences. Of course, such an environment can hardly be suggested as a model for Africa to imitate indiscriminately. Even if we want to, we simply cannot afford the cost. I have referred to the University of Florida model only to underscore the fact that the success of any serious scientific endeavour requires a critical mass of human resources. I recently looked through a random selection of 15 graduate catalogues of entomology departments in the USA and found that the average number of graduate faculty per department was 17. In Africa, by contrast, we have a truly dismal picture in which there are usually 3 entomologists (or less) in a faculty (school) of agriculture! This situation precludes the diversity of intellectual intercourse and cross-pollination which is essential to quality graduate training. Even if these few faculty are not burdened by the demands of under-graduate training, the best they can do is to pass their strengths as well as their weaknesses to their students in a frustrating cycle of intellectual in-breeding.

The Need for Supra-National Institutions

The truth is that African universities are, in fact, faced with a multitude of institutional handicaps, grossly inadequate resources and onerous demands for undergraduate training. Sad to say, some of these institutions are ill-equipped for even undergraduate education in science. Deprived of essential facilities, some of these institutions have been reduced to glorified high schools where brilliant men and women cram science rather than engage in innovative experimentation.

Cognisant of these constraints, it is my well-considered opinion that we must look beyond traditional strategies and tactics in our deliberations for a wherewithal for a sustainable capacity building for insect science leadership. Frankly, I believe that what we need is a supra-national institution that can provide the kind of broad-based curriculum which I have discussed earlier. African nations can pool their resources to create a center of true excellence at this supra-national institution. The logic for such an institution is simple and compelling. We need a sustainable capacity building for insect sciences and indeed for ALL sciences in Africa. Individual countries and universities lack the resources to provide such a capacity building. As things are, the resources at our universities are overburdened even for undergraduate training. Therefore, we ought to pool resources to achieve in concert what we are not able to achieve by separate efforts.

Building a Sustainable Capacity for Insect Science Leadership

We are all aware that the International Centre of Insect Physiology and Ecology (ICIPE), has provided truly outstanding leadership for science in Africa. As a graduate student, I recall many frustrations in my search for entomological journals from Africa. The *Insect Science and Its Application* arrived like a shock, even if a pleasant one, by a thunderbolt. I am not ashamed to say that every time I read that journal, I am filled with pride and emotions, not only that innovative research is taking place in Africa, but that it is being reported in an African journal. I visited the ICIPE in 1986 and was amazed at the ultra-modern facilities. A question that nagged my mind during that visit was why the Centre could not be expanded to provide first-class entomological graduate training for the whole of Africa? I was later to learn about the African Regional Postgraduate Programme in Insect Science (ARPPIS), a collaborative training scheme involving ICIPE and a number of African universities. With the success of ARPPIS, we already have a model in place at ICIPE for capacity building for insect science leadership in Africa. This model evolved around the peculiar needs of Africa and has already incorporated some of the strengths from other successful models in the world. I would suggest that the programme be expanded as necessary to meet the manpower needs for insect scientists in Africa. The next question is: How can this capacity be made sustainable?

Since only fools rush in where angels fear to tread, I will play the fool by stepping briefly into the murky path of African politics. Over two decades ago, Mrs. Indira Gandhi, the late Prime Minister of India, noted that the under-developed nations of the 20th century are those that did not climb aboard the Industrial Revolution of the early 19th century. She vowed that the next industrial revolution would not by-pass India. Whatever her inadequacies might have been, she made a consistently strong case for science education in India. Today, India is one of the twenty leading nations in science. In our lifetime, South Korea has been transformed from a Third World nation into an economic and industrial giant. They began by recognising their greatest asset — minds. They invested in science and technology and their harvest has been abundant. To see Mikhail Gorbachev seeking industrial cooperation (make that assistance) from South Korea is to see a serious people rewarded for their vision and sacrifice. A nation that invests in science and technology will reap the harvest of economic development.

What a sharp contrast to what obtains in most of Africa. With rare exceptions, what do we find in Africa? Take Nigeria, a nation of quite enormous resources. Slogans and acronyms! Operation Feed the Nation (OFN), Green Revolution (GR), Ethical Revolution (ER), War Against Indiscipline (WAI), Structural Adjustment Plan (SAP). The slogans and acronyms are endless. But nations are not built on acronyms, no matter how sweet and pleasing they sound. Napoleon once said, "We rule men with words". Very true, but it takes more than words to build a nation. If speeches alone would do, Nigeria would have been transformed into paradise. Talk, alone, is no remedy for starvation and kwashiorkor! Deafened by the myrmidons of hell, our rulers wasted and still waste our resources on white elephants in their so-called development plans that leave out Africa's greatest resources — minds! With the underdeveloped state of our science and technology, we have remained seemingly helpless victims of the vagaries of nature, having surrendered to a Philistine fatalism. For our intellectuals, scientists and non-scientists alike, life has become a prehensile struggle in intellectual and physical subsistence. Meanwhile, greener pastures continue to beckon: Saudi Arabia, Kuwait, the UK or the USA. A primoridal instinct in animals is to emigrate from an environment that threatens the survival of the species. A disproportionate number of the fittest are among the first to leave. But do our rulers care about the brain drain? If they do, they have a bizarre way of showing it. The last meeting of the Organisation of African Unity deliberated on every conceivable topic except science and technology!

Conclusions

We must remain resolute in the strive to create a sustainable insect science leadership in Africa. This resoluteness demands that we evolve innovative ways of making in-roads into the political process so that more of African resources can be allocated to science and technology. In practical terms, we may have to establish powerful lobby groups that can move through the corridors of power and influence decision-making. We must educate the politicians to the extent that they need to be educated. Similarly, we must recruit powerful members of the mass media to join us in this great task of selling science to our leaders. Our business men and women must be induced to give to the cause of science. Happily, wealthy people have a love for immortality. One of the ways they can achieve immortality is to get monuments named after them. So, I propose that we name academic buildings or campus streets for people who would donate generously to academic or research institutions. These suggestions do not preclude the continued benefits from the donor agencies whose generosity has sustained the excellence with which we have come to associate ICIPE. But we can hardly overemphasise the need for greater involvement of local financial resources in creating a scientific/technological base for African development. Such an involvement would blaze a new trail in the annals of education and development in Africa. Would this be an easy task? Not by any means. It would be tempting to yield to a mental chloroform that anesthetises us into the acceptance that whatever had not been done before, cannot be done. But we must not.

Today, ICIPE stands as a brilliant testimony that with sufficient vision, courage and unflagging zeal, new things can be done. With a fresh and renewed vision of the gargantuan task before us, we can indeed embark on innovative ways of bringing the glorious vision to pass.

INNOVATIVE LINKAGES OF UNIVERSITIES AND RESEARCH INSTITUTES: ICIPE'S EXPERIENCE

Z.T. Dabrowski
*Institutional Building and
Interactive Research Unit (IBIRU)
The International Centre of Insect
Physiology and Ecology (ICIPE)
Nairobi, Kenya*

Introduction

Participants of the Regional Workshop on Training Needs for Agricultural Research in Eastern and Southern Africa, held in Arusha in July, 1987, lamented that "the most conspicuous characteristic of National Agricultural Research and Training Systems (NARS) in the region is their weakness". For example,

- They are staffed by young and/or inadequately trained persons. Less than 8% of indigenous scientists in 10 countries have received training to Ph.D. level and about 57% do not possess a postgraduate qualification (see Table 1).

- Many NARSs in the region are understaffed and some rely very heavily on donor-sponsored expatriate personnel.

- Nearly all countries in the region do not make sufficient budgetary provisions for recurrent and capital development expenditure for agricultural research. Consequently, there has been very little meaningful research. Those countries with strong research programmes seem to be over-dependent on donor agencies.

- The socio-economic environment in some countries is not conducive to research. This results in considerable brain drain and low output. (Anon., 1987).

The Workshop also noted that cooperation between national agricultural research systems and university faculties of agriculture in the same country was not sufficient to allow for optimal utilisation of staff in NARSs for training. Within the region as a whole, there were opportunities for cooperation in training among universities through exchange of staff and students (e.g., the Inter-University Council for East Africa between Uganda, Kenya and Tanzania). However, such potential cooperation lacked strong political and institutional backing.

The participants concluded that at that time there was no clear formal regional cooperative training programme, either at the undergraduate or postgraduate level, and there were no cross-border regional training donor-assisted projects for postgraduate studies in agriculture. In the past, such projects have been quite successful. For example, the Rockefeller Foundation financed a programme for staff development in Kenya, Uganda and Tanzania (the former University of East Africa), and the regional Masters' Programme in Agricultural Economics was funded by the Ford Foundation at Makerere University in the early seventies. Many nationals presently holding senior managerial positions in NARCs and universities in the region were trained or achieved their career development through such projects (Anon., 1987).

TABLE 1: QUALIFICATIONS OF RESEARCH STAFF IN NARSs OF COUNTRIES IN EASTERN AND SOUTHERN AFRICA

Country	B.Sc.	M.Sc.	Ph.D.	Total
Botswana	7	11	2	20
Ethiopia	129	59	14	202
Kenya	246	205	25	470
Lesotho	6	11	0	17
Rwanda	16	6	2	24
Somalia	33	7	0	40
Tanzania (TARO)	127	60	17	204
Uganda	106	78	16	200
Zambia	51	33	4	88
Zimbabwe	109	54	32	195
Total	830	524	112	1465
Percentage	56.6	35.7	7.6	100

Source: Anon., 1987

The participating deans and directors of national research systems and international organizations made a number of recommendations to improve the postgraduate training. These include "establishing schools of graduate studies where they do not exist" and encouraging "more collaboration between national agricultural research institutions and national universities in the training of postgraduate students so as to make maximum use of all qualified and experienced personnel within the country". Their observations and recommendations were later confirmed by all major international bodies interested in higher education in Africa, including the World Bank's agencies (Contant, 1984; AFAA, 1991).

Models of Research Centre-University Relations in Education Programmes

Some international donors' missions undertaken between 1987-1991 to the sub-Saharan universities confirmed the facts cited above: there is an acute shortage of postgraduate training opportunities in Africa. We at ARPPIS agree with their observations that some of the larger donors supporting research have concentrated on financing long-term training overseas and short-term training in international research centres. Regarding existing opportunities for M.Sc. training, our three ARPPIS Missions to Southern, Western and Eastern/North-Eastern Africa reported, however, that manpower resources and research facilities for various disciplines of science are scarce and scattered across the African continent, but they are not absent (Siwela and Gopo, 1989; Egwuatu, *et al.*, 1990; Siwela and Dabrowski, 1991). The reports confirmed observations made by Nwa and colleagues (1990) and published by the Association of African Universities (AAU),that the present economic crisis particularly adversely affected the universities and their postgraduate programmes (see also Djangmah in these Proceedings). Identification of mechanisms harnessing the strengths and abilities of these scarce resources at sub-Saharan universities and research institutions has been on the agenda of all major meetings concerning higher education in Africa organized during the last ten years (Anon., 1987 and 1988; SPAAR, 1987; World Bank, 1988 and 1989; ARPPIS, in press; AFAA, 1991; FAO, 1991).

Three major models are currently being developed to improve higher education in the tropics with aspects to commend them.

- Specific departments in African universities have been identified by several donor organisations for special support. This support, both financial and through the secondment of staff from overseas, goes into creating regional centres of excellence. However, these centres still utilise only the staff and facilities of African universities and will not draw upon any research centres outside the university system.

For example, the School of Information Studies for Africa (SISA) is a regional training centre established in 1990 with the assistance of the International Development Research Centre of Canada (IDRC) and UNESCO. Located at Addis Ababa University (Ethiopia), it offers an M.Sc. in Information Science. SISA's faculty includes: four local staff (with a rank of lecturer and above); three expatriates (Professor; Associate Professor/Reader); and Assistant Professor/Senior Lecturer), all based full-time at Addis Ababa University. The University of Dar es Salaam (Tanzania) has successfully run and administered a regional M.Sc. programme in Water Resources Engineering supported by the African Network of Scientific and Technological Institutions (ANSTI).

- Collaboration within the African region between universities and research centres is a second model. There have been several successful collaborative programmes of limited scope, established in different parts of the developing world. The Rockefeller International Maize and Wheat Improvement (CIMMYT) has had close links with Kasetsart University in Thailand, and the International Rice Research Institute (IRRI) has a graduate training programme with the University of the Philippines at Los Banos. In Africa, the International Institute of Tropical Agriculture (IITA) has an association with the University of Ibadan, Nigeria. In all these examples, the objective is to offer the facilities of the research centre to graduate students of the collaborating university. But as valuable as these collaborative training programmes are, they are limited in geographical impact and are based on relationships between only two partners, and will therefore depend on the qualities and strengths of only two institutions (Smalley, 1987). In some of these programmes, there is a clear separation of the role of university and the centre as illustrated by the following example: "to be eligible for selection, candidates must be enrolled in a university anywhere in the world, financially supported while they are fulfilling the academic requirements for M.Sc. or Ph.D. degree, and must have completed all the course work" (IITA, 1990).

The African Biosciences Network was established in 1981 bringing together individual biologists as well as regional and international research organizations. The network supports training courses and workshops on insect pests and vectors, but does not support graduate training programmes (Bekoe, 1984).

African universities have a valuable tradition of academic work, but there are international research centres on the continent which are not universities, but which do have the facilities and expertise to supervise higher degree research. High-level and excellent degree research requires both an academic tradition and teaching, as well as the facilities for modern research. By universities and research centres remaining separate, the opportunities for graduate training in Africa will remain limited. By coming together in a collaborative programme, the possibilities for quality graduate training are greatly increased.

- The third model represents research centres having a degree-awarding status within the national laws but outside the national university system. Such an example is the Indian Agricultural Research Institute (IARI) which was founded in 1923; the status changed to that of a deemed university in 1955, after which both M.Sc. and Ph.D. programmes were introduced. Staff at the Institute are employed to teach and carry out research, and all students must achieve a minimum grade before beginning their research (see Y.P. Singh in these Proceedings). The All India Institute of Medical Science was established in 1956 as a deemed University, with the same overall objectives and structure as the IARI.

> The Instituto Venezolano de Investigaciones Cientificas (IVIC), described during this Conference by its director, Professor Horacio Venegas, was originally founded in 1954 as an institute for neurological research. In 1959, its mandate was widened to include all the sciences and such applied areas as the oil industry and computer science. A Centre for Postgraduate Studies was established at IVIC in 1971 by an Act of Parliament. The Centre was based at IVIC rather than at a Venezuelan University because IVIC already had the necessary staff facilities and expertise. Between 1973-91, the Institute graduated 454 students with the M.Sc. degree and 67 with the Ph.D. (Venegas, 1991). Approximately 50% of the graduates are working at universities and higher learning institutions in Venezuela.

The African Regional Postgraduate Programme in Insect Science (ARPPIS)

ARPPIS AS A MODEL FOR COLLABORATIVE EDUCATION

As Professor T.R. Odhiambo, Director of the ICIPE and Chairman of the ARPPIS Academic Board, has mentioned in his welcoming remarks to this Conference, there was an ICIPE African Committee initiative in 1978 to recommend the establishment of an international postgraduate course in insect science in Africa in collaboration with African universities (Odhiambo, 1991). The programme was endorsed during the meeting of representatives of nine African universities, ICIPE, international organisations and donors in Bellagio in 1981. The African Regional Postgraduate Programme in Insect Science (ARPPIS) was formally established in 1983, and after nine years of existence, may serve as a positive example of innovative cooperation between the present 21 African member universities and ICIPE. (See Figure 1). Six other universities have expressed their desire to join ARPPIS, including those from Egypt, Morocco, Senegal, Burundi and Rwanda. The ARPPIS is entirely based in Africa and its training programme has special relevance since it offers students the opportunity to research into African insect pests and vectors *in situ*. The programme is open to students from throughout the continent and provides a new learning and research environment (although still within the tropics), away from the students' home, and away from any distracting administrative responsibilities. Finally, the degree courses are completed within the specified period because the students have access to the facilities and staff of the ICIPE.

ARPPIS is presented as a novel contribution to graduate training in developing countries and as such it serves as a model for similar collaborative programmes elsewhere in the tropics. It can also serve as a model for training in other scientific disciplines.

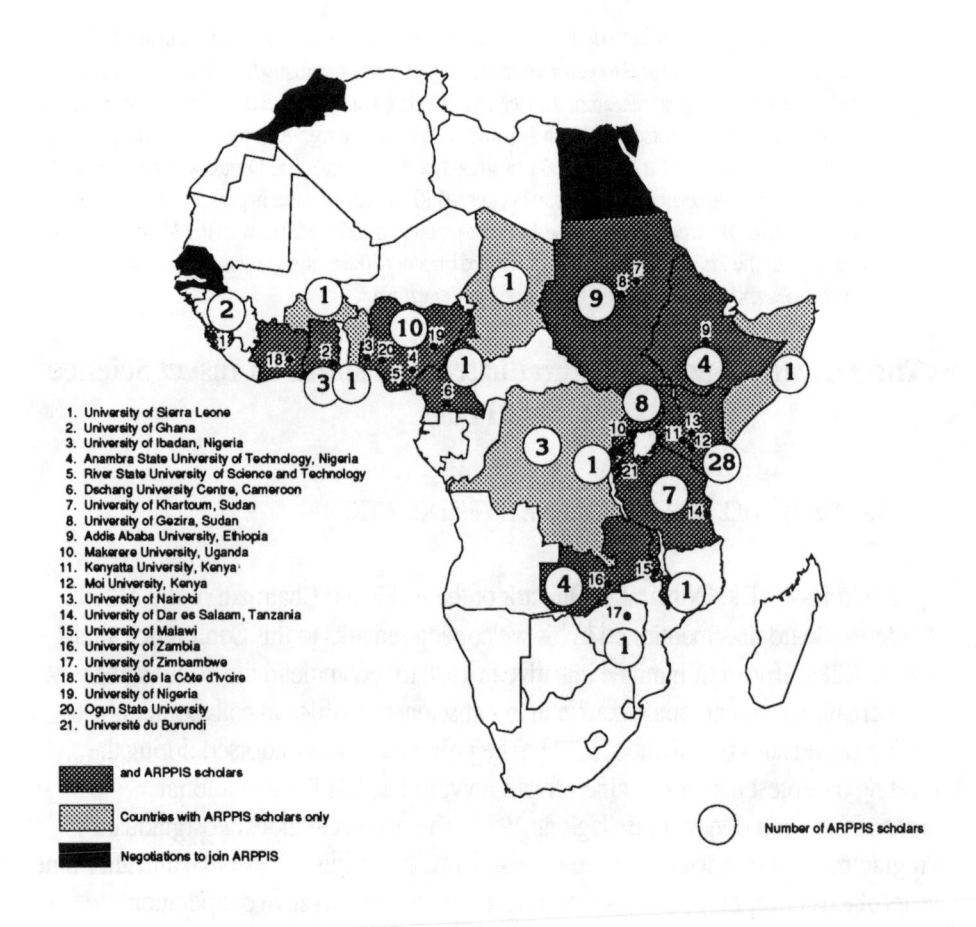

FIGURE 1: THE ARPPIS NETWORK

ACADEMIC ADMINISTRATION OF ARPPIS

The Academic Coordinator of ARPPIS, who is responsible for the day-to-day administration of the network, is located at the ICIPE, but the effectiveness of the programme depends on the efficiency of communication with the universities. Each participating university has nominated a senior member of faculty to represent its interests on the ARPPIS Academic Board and it is the Board member who forms the vital link in transmitting the ideas of his university to ARPPIS and those of ARPPIS back to this university. The Board member is the guarantee of action and of response.

The Academic Board is the senior decision-making body of ARPPIS, and meets twice each year. It brings together representatives from each university and from the ICIPE. The Board is responsible for the selection of students, the approval of coursework and research projects and all other academic matters referred to it.

The student selection process balances three different considerations: the academic qualifications, the availability of facilities and supervision, and the need to achieve an equitable geographical spread of ARPPIS students. Applicants to ARPPIS must have a good first degree in an agricultural, veterinary or zoological discipline. The applicant must also have a significant background in entomology.

There have inevitably been some problems in harmonising the regulations of 21 universities for registration and particularly for residential requirements. These problems were recognised at an early stage and no major attempt has been made to alter the Senate regulations of any participating university. Rather, ARPPIS has been presented as a special case with a request that demands for prolonged residency on the campus of the registering university should be waived. Satisfactory progress is being made in the case of some universities.

THE ACADEMIC PROGRAMME

The three-year programme for each class includes an initial six-month semester of coursework, a two-year period for research and a final six months for the preparation and submission of the thesis. All these activities are carried out at the ICIPE. All coursework is compulsory and examined and involves six examined mandatory courses and three supplementary courses. The university systems of most English-speaking African countries are modelled upon the traditions of the United Kingdom. That tradition does not normally involve coursework in Ph.D. programmes. Indeed, the ARPPIS coursework does not contribute to the final evaluation of the student; that is done by the presentation of a thesis and by an oral examination. The coursework was introduced because ARPPIS students come from a variety of academic and cultural backgrounds and the courses are intended to set a uniform level of understanding in core areas of entomology, and to orientate the students to possible areas of research.

The course coordinators and lecturers are drawn from participating university faculty and from the ICIPE scientific staff. For the 1991 semester, three course coordinators came from universities and three from the ICIPE. Lecturers from both the universities and the ICIPE are internationally recognised authorities in their disciplines.

Two areas of concern have arisen out of the coursework semester. Firstly, ARPPIS has found that most students have a poor background in taxonomy, physiology, biochemistry, biostatistics and biological control. Seventy-two of the 86 ARPPIS students had previously studied for their Masters Degree at an African university, and it must be reluctantly concluded that these Masters programmes did not present courses of sufficiently high quality in these areas of entomology.

Secondly, it has proved difficult to identify from the university faculty, ecologists able to present a high-level quantitative course in insect ecology. By contrast, in the 1991 semester, Professor H. Morgan of the University of Sierra Leone (a leading insect ecologist) offered ARPPIS students a two-week course on general advanced ecology, and Prof. J. Elkinton of the University of Massachusetts, a two-week course on quantitative ecology, supported by the ICIPE ecologists during field and laboratory (computers) practicals.

THE RESEARCH PROJECT

The research project of each student is developed by the student in consultation with ICIPE scientists during the teaching semester. The project selected must be one for which the ICIPE has expertise and facilities, for one of the basic understandings of ARPPIS is that the ICIPE will provide day-to-day supervision of the students on behalf of the registering university. Each student has a supervisory committee of three, one internal supervisor from the registering university and two external supervisors from the ICIPE.

The Ph.D. research projects selected have been distributed almost equally between original and adaptive research, and are all on major African insect pests or vectors being studied in the appropriate context. Mention has already been made of the need to train insect scientists in the objectives and methods of biological control. Six ARPPIS students are working on biological control projects but there have been problems in identifying university faculty to supervise the work.

The above highlights the need to train such scientists, the problems of doing so and the benefits of a network where expertise can be shared. All networks are built on mutual confidence and in a training network this is crucial, because the qualifications and future of the students are involved. The participating universities must be assured of the standard of the research work of their students and that the students will pay short visits to their registering institution. In the majority of cases the period between submission of thesis and examination took between 9-20 months, with exceptional cases requiring more than 24-29 months.

The above discussion shows that the ARPPIS has a unique structural collaborative network, combining the strengths and ambitions of both an international research centre and of the African Participating Universities. Since 1983, both the ICIPE and the Participating Universities have achieved a great deal together, through agreement and implementation of the present ARPPIS Ph.D. programme.

EVALUATION OF THE ARPPIS PH.D. PROGRAMME

In spite of its many strong points, the Task Force appointed in 1987 on the Future Development of Graduate Training at the ICIPE nevertheless concluded that the success of ARPPIS in the past has been realised with a structure that has been inherently unstable, and one on which further development should not be dependent. The reasons for the instability, and lack of proper foundation for future development, were identified as follows:

- problems experienced by ARPPIS students in completing the requirements of their respective Participating Universities;

- difficulties in obtaining adequate and effective guidance and feedback from their university supervisors;

- long residency requirements by some Participating Universities;

- dependence on individual university officers, who often change during the time of the students' pursuance of degree programmes at the ICIPE; and

- difficulties of particular universities in accepting parts of the curriculum on which university participation has been minimal, or where they have little expertise (ICIPE, 1991).

ARPPIS is continuously being evaluated by visiting academicians, politicians and donor representatives. Participants of the Seventh General Conference of the Association of Faculties of Agriculture in Africa, meeting in June, 1991, in Nairobi made the following observations on ARPPIS:

- "... The Founding Fathers of the Institute School (ARPPIS) are commended for their foresight. The research topics made available to the visitors are very relevant to the African situation. The most outstanding research (of the ARPPIS) students is that on mosquitoes. The Institute seems to be well equipped for the research topics undertaken". *Prof. S.C. Achinewhu, Dean, Rivers State University of Science and Technology, Port Harcourt, Nigeria.*

- "... I was extremely fascinated with the remarkable research facilities of the institute and more important, the thought-provoking qualities of the staff and students who are deeply involved in a myriad of research activities on worldwide insect problems... I was very much pleased with the tenacity and dedication of these young people in their attempt to find answers to tomorrow's insect problems. I was equally thrilled to find a lady at the institute, who is equally making a major contribution to the role of women in research and development". *Dr. J.L. Tommy, Dean, University of Sierra Leone.*

- "... It was a pleasure for me to visit ICIPE once again after several years. I was immensely impressed by the development that has taken place, especially the institution of ARPPIS. The ARPPIS Postgraduate Training Programme to Ph.D. degree level attracting students from all over Africa is playing a vital role in research capability building, a major prerequisite for high-calibre research in Africa. As Deans of Faculties of Agriculture in Africa, the least we can do is to pledge our unequivocal support and collaboration in ICIPE's efforts. The group of ARPPIS trainees we met looked very happy, contented, enthusiastic and knowledgeable about their respective research projects. One wishes more students could be recruited into the programme to accelerate the achievement of a critical mass of quality researchers to generate new technologies for IPM". *Prof. J.S. Mugerwa, Dean, Makerere University, Uganda.*

- "...I am highly impressed by the research projects of the ARPPIS students and the facilities available at ICIPE. I believe that the institution's objectives will help the "true" development of academic work in Africa and assist in finding solutions to some of the social and academic problems in the continent [affected by brain-drain of its academicians]. *Dr. O. Onayemi, Coordinator, Food and Nutrition Project, Association of African Universities, Accra, Ghana.*

- "...[ARPPIS] students are bright, intelligent and apparently deeply motivated. The research projects they have been working on have evident relevance on health and crops. They merit congratulations and encouragement for conducting their research work. This [programme] should be known by the scientific community, especially in Africa". *Prof. P. Ndabeneze, Dean, University of Burundi (translation from French).*

- *Professor Moussa Fall, Directeur de l'Ecole Nationale Superieure d'Agriculture de Thies, Republic du Senegal* adds that "... ARPPIS activities should be [further] extended to Francophone countries in West Africa".

- *Professor K. El Shazly, retired President of AFAA and Dean, University of Alexandria* "was very impressed by the facilities available and at the method of multidisciplinary approach [by ARPPIS students] in solving problems of vector control using biocontrol [methods]. The standard of research of the few students that I was able to meet, the methodology and the results presented were outstanding. I am worried about the evaluation of their contribution to the research and development in their home countries. I hope [some] programmes could be devoted toward a follow-up of their activities in their home countries".

- *Professor M.L. Firdaway, the present AFAA President and Principal, Institut Agronomique et Veterinaire, Hassan II, Rabat, Morocco,* summarized the Dean's opinion in the following way: "It is the kind of network formula I would like to see expanded in other fields and disciplines where many universities could join their efforts. Very good facilities, flexibility and quality".

The Third Periodic External Review Team, selected from internationally recognised scientists, managers and representatives of donors reviewing the ICIPE and ARPPIS in March 1990, stated that they were "... impressed by the quality of research and motivation of the ARPPIS students, and ... would like to commend ICIPE for having spearheaded this innovative approach for the practical training of applied entomologists for the ever-increasing demand at the national level".

CONTRIBUTIONS OF ARPPIS GRADUATES

Dr. C.G. Nderitu, Director of the Kenyan Agricultural Research Institute (KARI) acknowledged that "more than a dozen indigenous Kenyans who have been through the ARPPIS Programme are teaching at local Universities, conducting research in KARI's research centres, sister institutes, Ministries, and are also working within ICIPE. Besides the generation of qualified manpower, the project research work being conducted by ARPPIS students has got much relevance to our Kenyan situation. Most of the project work is undertaken in Kenya and it directly or indirectly makes available basic and applied information pertaining to the problem being investigated. For instance, a lot of information regarding biology, ecology and control strategies of one of the introduced cassava pests, cassava green mite *Mononychellus tanajoa* (Bondar), has been generated and it is very useful in designing future management strategies of this pest. This is just an example of many areas in which ARPPIS students have conducted research and I hope more will be done in fields in which we are currently experiencing problems" (Nderitu, in press).

There are numerous examples of how graduates of the first five ARPPIS classes (1983-1987) have already contributed to innovations in such areas as curriculum development within their universities; redesigning the teaching courses and practicals based on ARPPIS-taught courses; and research and technology development for IPM. I wish to give only one example, that of Dr. J.H.P. Nyeko (1983 ARPPIS Class), presently Principal Research Entomologist at the Tsetse Control Department, Uganda. He is the only specialist with a Ph.D. in vector management in Uganda. This fact is a major drawback in tsetse control activities in Uganda. Although tsetse control forms a department of its own in the Ministry of Animal Industry and Fisheries, it seriously lacks qualified entomologists. Currently there are 14 B.Sc. graduates working in the department and three of these are doing their M.Sc. training in entomology. These scientists are not specialists and they are unable to collect scientific data on the ecology, behaviour, trapping response and the vectorial capacity of the nine tsetse species in the country. This fact has limited tsetse control activities in Uganda to insecticide application only. Recently, however, Lancien traps are being experimented with by Dr. Nyeko in the Sleeping Sickness (SS) areas of Busoga.

Dr. Nyeko informed participants of the ARPPIS Graduate Conference that "on the side of animal trypanosomiasis, we have recently carried out surveys in several districts in the country to determine the disease prevalence and the trypanosome species involved. There has been tremendous improvement in the surveillance, detection and treatment of infections in humans. This has led to a significant reduction in human SS cases from over 6700 in 1987 to less than 500 in 1989/1990" (Nyeko, in press).

These evaluations confirm that the contribution the ARPPIS is making to human resource development in insect science, including training for integrated pest and vector management in Africa, is unprecedented.

At the same time, the overall contribution of 30-35 resident ARPPIS students attached to ICIPE research programmes is a distinct benefit to the Centre itself. ICIPE

Programme Leaders and Unit Heads have all noted the contribution ARPPIS students are making to the achievements of ICIPE's strategic research objectives, and it is expected that Ph.D. students will significantly increase the research output of individual supervisors. Recent surveys showed that 2-3 more joint publications are produced annually by the ARPPIS students' supervisors than by other ICIPE scientists.

Conclusion

The academic training for African scientists both at the master's and doctorate levels must be relevant to the national programme and development needs of their countries. It must be well planned, be of high quality and be providable within a reasonable time scale. There is the additional requirement that the training must be sensitive to the needs of the student. There is a difference between learning and understanding. To thoroughly understand a concept or a problem, the information must be presented in the cultural context of the student. By seeing and understanding a problem in the appropriate context, a student is more likely to be able to relate his knowledge and expertise to the needs of his own ecological and socio-economic environment (Smalley, 1987).

The pest and vector problems of Africa, and of the whole developing world, are peculiar to the countries concerned, and yet so many students go outside the tropics for their degree training. They go to benefit from the knowledge and expertise in specialist departments in overseas universities and also because funds are available for overseas study. These benefits cannot be ignored. University training is designed to enable students to identify, analyse and discuss a problem and the processes learnt outside the tropics are equally applicable to problems in the students' home country once the student returns. Experience has shown that students trained abroad do indeed receive an excellent education and develop a wider outlook on their work than may be achieved from continuous training in a *single* local university.

But developing countries are, rightly, in a hurry to solve their own problems and there is a need for more of their young scientists to have the opportunity to gain relevant research experience in their own agricultural and ecological systems. As Dr. S. Kyamanywa (1983 ARPPIS Class) observed during the first ARPPIS Graduates Conference in December 1990,

> "the postgraduate training abroad served well but had one in-built disadvantage, that those trained in those countries found it difficult to re-orient themselves towards the Ugandan (African) needs and priorities. This has had two main impacts. Firstly, the graduates from abroad find themselves more comfortable

working in developed countries whose problems are familiar, hence encouraging the brain drain phenomenon. Secondly, the graduates, at the time of their creative growth and innovation, are exposed to principles and problems of developed systems, so that those who come to teach in our University just perpetuate the same principles. Not that the principles are bad; no. They are just not suitable for our situations" (Kyamanywa, in press).

The ARPPIS has been presented here as a novel contribution to graduate training in Africa, which has proved that competent professionals can also be trained in the South to serve the South. In the ninth year of its existence "it is impossible to imagine ARPPIS without the ICIPE and the ICIPE without ARPPIS". The ARPPIS may serve and is always serving as a model for similar collaborative programmes in insect science in Africa and elsewhere in the tropics, and as a model for training in other scientific disciplines.

References

AFAA. 1991. Recommendations of the Seventh General Conference on Agricultural Research and Development in Africa. 10-16 June 1991, Nairobi, Kenya.

Anon. 1987. Summary, Observations and Recommendations from Regional Workshop on Training Needs for Agricultural Research in Eastern and Southern Africa. Sponsored by International Development Research Centre (IDRC) and The International Institute of Tropical Agriculture (IITA), 20-24 July 1987, Arusha, Tanzania.

Anon. 1988. Symposium on Graduate Studies in Eastern and Southern Africa. Second Meeting of Deans/Directors/ Coordinators of Graduate Studies, 8-12 February 1988, Gaborone, Botswana.

ARPPIS (in press). *Proceedings of the International Conference on Capacity Building in Insect Science in Africa: Field Experience and Evaluation of the Impact of ARPPIS.* ICIPE World Headquarters, Duduville, 3-6 December 1990, Nairobi, Kenya. The African Regional Postgraduate Programme in Insect Science (ARPPIS).

Bekoe, D.A. 1984. *The African Biosciences Network*, Rivers State University of Science and Technology, Port Harcourt, Nigeria. *Public Lectures 1983-1984*, pp 16-20.

Contant, R.B. 1984. Linking agricultural research and higher agricultural education: a partnership for success. *Proceedings AFAA 5th General Conference on Food Security in Africa*, 22-28 April 1984, Swaziland. AFAA; Rabat, Morocco.

Egwuatu, R.I., Morgan, H.G., Dabrowski, Z.T., and Olaniran, Y.A.O. 1990. Report on the Mission to Nigeria, Ghana and the Republic of Cameroon, 4-25th February 1990, presented to the ARPPIS Academic Board, 7th June 1990.

FAO. 1991. The Role of Universities in National Agricultural Research Systems. Highlights of FAO Expert Consultation, 19-22 March 1991. FAO Research and Technology Development Division, Rome.

ICIPE. 1991. Graduate Training in Insect Science at the ICIPE: Planning Document. Revised Draft Mimeo, May 1991, The International Centre of Insect Physiology and Ecology, Nairobi.

IITA. 1990. Graduate Research Fellowship Programme. International Institute of Tropical Agriculture, November, 1990.

Kyamanywa, S. (in press). The need of African universities for new and innovative teaching methods and curricula in insect science: The role of ARPPIS and the Ugandan experience. *Proceedings of the International Conference on Capacity Building in Insect Science in Africa: Field Experience and Evaluation of the Impact of ARPPIS*, ICIPE World Headquarters, 3-6 December 1990, Duduville, Nairobi. ARPPIS, Nairobi.

Nderitu, C.G. (in press). The relevance of ARPPIS training for national agricultural research systems in Kenya: The Kenyan experience. *ibid.*

Nwa, E.U., Houenou P., and Sackey, M.D. 1990. Graduate Education and R & D in African Universities. Report submitted to the Association of African Universities, May 1990, Accra, Ghana.

Nyeko, J.H.P. (in press). Meeting needs of national programmes in advanced training in integrated management of tsetse in Uganda. *Proceedings of the International Conference on Capacity Building in Insect Science in Africa: Field Experience and Evaluation of the Impact of ARPPIS*, ICIPE World Headquarters, 3-6 December 1990, Duduville, Nairobi. ARPPIS, Nairobi.

Odhiambo, T.R. 1991. Welcome remarks. In these Proceedings.

Singh, Y.P. 1991. Role of research centres in postgraduate training in India. In these Proceedings.

Siwela, A. and Dabrowski, Z.T. 1991. Report on the Mission to Identify the ARPPIS M.Sc. Sub-Regional Centre for Eastern and North-Eastern Africa, submitted to the ARPPIS Academic Board, 2nd June 1991.

Siwela, A. and Gopo, J.M. 1989. Report on the ARPPIS Mission to Malawi, Lesotho, Botswana, Swaziland, Zambia and Zimbabwe to discuss the Sub-Regional M.Sc. Programme in Insect Science; presented to the ARPPIS Academic Board on 5th December 1989.

Smalley, M.E. 1987. A model for a regional collaborative training programme in insect science. *Insect Science and Its Application*, **8**, 943-950.

SPAAR. 1991. *Guidelines for Strengthening National Agricultural Research Systems in Sub-Saharan Africa*. Special Program for African Agricultural Research and ISNAR; The World Bank, Washington, D.C.

Vanegas, H. F. 1991. The role of research centres in postgraduate training in South America. In these Proceedings.

The World Bank. 1988. *Education in Sub-Saharan Africa: Policies for Adjustment, Revitalization and Expansion*. The World Bank, Washington, D.C.

The World Bank. 1989. *Sub-Saharan Africa: From Crisis to Sustainable Growth*. The International Bank for Reconstruction and Development (The World Bank), Washington, D.C.

THE PROPOSED ICIPE GRADUATE SCHOOL: CONCEPT AND RATIONALE

T. R. Odhiambo
*Director, The International Centre
of Insect Physiology and Ecology (ICIPE)
Nairobi, Kenya*

The mandate of the International Centre of Insect Physiology and Ecology (ICIPE), since its establishment in April 1970, has always been on a twin-track: the development of technologically feasible, economically affordable, and ecologically sustainable pest management technologies for internationally important tropical pests and insect disease vectors; and to greatly enhance scientific capacities in the tropics, particularly in Africa where the ICIPE has its roots, through high-level training and research cooperation. This mandate has been graphically enunciated in a most apposite manner by one of the founding fathers, Dr. Victor Rabinowitch, in a Special Guest Lecture he gave on 14th April 1985, during the ICIPE Annual Research Conference in Nairobi, Kenya (Rabinowitch, 1986). He described ICIPE's overall mandate in these terms:

> "In many respects, the October 1969 planning meeting [for the establishment of ICIPE, held at the University of Nairobi, Kenya], bringing together insect physiologists, chemists, geneticists, ecologists, and scientists concerned not only with fundamental research but also with the application of insect research to the solution of practical problems of agriculture and health in Africa was unique. For one thing, the focus was on Africa, a continent new to many, if not all, the participants. For another, the emphasis was on international scientific cooperation for the ultimate purpose of solving critical development problems, providing more and better food to African people and protecting them more adequately from disease. It was clearly understood, indeed stressed, that building up African capabilities to deal with insect problems in the region was fundamental to the development of an institute."

This was, indeed, an ambitious, far-reaching goal for a new institute rooted in a continent most devastatingly unlinked from the contemporary frontiers of scientific advancement worldwide.

ICIPE's Achievements in Its First Two Decades

The first two decades of ICIPE's existence have, however, demonstrated that this goal is achievable. The Centre has made tremendous multi-disciplinary advances in the understanding of the major pest groups on which it is concentrating its research effort, leading to the design and development of new technologies for pest management. The ICIPE has pioneered the mechanisms for bringing together leading academies of science to share in creating a new forum for international cooperation in science-led development. Such a mechanism was subsequently utilised in establishing the International Institute of Applied Systems Analysis (IIASA), based in Laxenberg, Austria and the International Foundation for Science (IFS), headquartered in Stockholm, Sweden. The Centre attracts many postdoctoral research fellows who are selected on a competitive basis from around the world, and who have always made a substantial proportion of the ICIPE international staff from its very inception.

Among African universities and research institutions, a regular postdoctoral research fellowship scheme does not exist, but a few are now seriously considering its potential. The ICIPE postdoctoral scheme has created a considerable awareness of tropical insect problems in many parts of the world. This awareness is responsible in a significant way for several institutions now being founded in developed countries using the ICIPE as a close model. Examples of such institutes are the Centre for Insect Science, established in 1990 at the University of Arizona, Tucson; and the Centre for Tropical Pest Management, founded in Australia this year as a collaborative project between the Commonwealth Science and Industrial Research Organisation (CSIRO) and several universities with strong interests in tropical and sub-tropical pest management.

Furthermore, the ICIPE has pioneered the establishment of thorough-going partnership networks in areas where the Centre has undoubted competence. Such networks include: the Network on Financial and Administrative Management of Research Projects in Eastern and Southern Africa **(FAMESA)**; the Pest Management Research and Development (R & D) Network **(PESTNET)**, where national research and extension services are partners; and the African Regional Postgraduate Programme in Insect Science **(ARPPIS)**, in which selected participating universities in Africa are partners. Such achievements, in circumstances in Africa currently inimical to vigorous intellectual and scientific communities, is instructive, and points to the potential of quantum achievements in the medium-term future, as a result of a progressively more sensitised African geopolitical and policy leadership.

A Vision for the Future

The ICIPE therefore dares to envision, by the year 2000, to have firmly established itself as the premier insect R & D institute in the tropical world (ICIPE, 1991a). It will express this premier position in four leadership areas.

- *First*, it will have consolidated its capacity to undertake the whole range of mission-oriented R & D activities from basic fundamental research, to applied research, to technology development, and to technology validation and large-scale demonstration by the year 2000.

- *Second*, it will have implemented a comprehensive approach to understanding the major insect targets all the way from their population ecology and host-insect relationships to cellular and molecular events.

- *Third*, the ICIPE will have established a family of R&D institutions composed of *(i)* the ICIPE headquarters research establishment concentrating on cell and molecular biosciences, biotechnology, and behavioural sciences; *(ii)* field research stations located in key agro-ecological zones in Kenya (representing similar ecologies elsewhere in the tropics) which will concentrate on population studies, host-insect relations, technology development, and social science interface research; *(iii)* collaborating institutions carefully selected in Africa, South-East Asia, and Latin America and the Caribbean through a cohesive pan-tropical PESTNET, concerned primarily with interactive technology development and validation for their own specific agro-ecologies, and its demonstration under these circumstances; and *(iv)* a network of high-level education and training institutions in tropical insect science, whose apex will be the **ICIPE Graduate School.**

- *Fourth*, the consolidation of a worldwide ICIPE-led "invisible college", consisting of active insect R & D scientists who have graduated from the ICIPE Graduate School within the framework of ARPPIS; former postdoctoral research fellows, research associates, professional fellows, and visiting scientists; and existing R & D cooperating research scientists.

The synergistic impact of such a functional collegial relationship can be immense in advancing the horizons of insect science and its application to the effective management of insect populations. This vision is writ large; but the ICIPE will, in actualizing it, know that it has first-class partners in Africa and throughout the world, and that it has created an R & D capacity in the tropical world to take its rightful place in the task of implementing this visionary yet practical strategy.

The ICIPE vision in terms of the ICIPE Graduate School, in its contextual framework as part-and-parcel of the ARPPIS network, reminds us of what the late Rector of the United Nations University, Dr. Soedjatmoko of Indonesia, had to tell us in his speech to the National Assembly of Educators, meeting in Washington, D.C., in May 1984 (Fenton, 1990).

> "... It seems clear to me that all countries – developed or underdeveloped, East or West of the ideological divide – are all ill-prepared to deal with the swiftly changing, enormously complex, and increasingly competitive world of tomorrow. Finding the means to prepare the whole of the global society for such a world is therefore essential. As I look to the next century, I am more and more convinced that it will be the capacity to learn – and in particular to learn from each other – which, more than any other single factor, will determine the viability, autonomy and integrity of all societies."

The ARPPIS programme has succeeded, in a supreme way, to bring out the sense of curiosity and the ability to improvise by its scholars that enable them to meet major challenges in working in the African environment, and to be excited about making scientific contributions to the horrendous development task in Africa. It is most reassuring, therefore, to find that none of the ARPPIS graduates have so far left Africa, and that they are still practising their profession.

What then are the unique strengths of ARPPIS; and what new dimension will the proposed ICIPE Graduate School bring to the new partnership between a consortium of African universities and an advanced research and education institute, the ICIPE?

The Factors for Success in ARPPIS

ARPPIS embodies at least five characteristics which, in combination, build an aura of success and singularity in this network which does not accompany other cooperative arrangements for postgraduate education elsewhere.

- *First*, there is a strong linkage between an advanced research and education centre (which brings to the partnership its strength in priority R & D in a field directly relevant to the tropics, as well as its worldwide linkages in the same area) and a consortium of African universities (which bring to the partnership their collective interest in advancing tropical insect science, as well as their commitment to high-level staff development in the field). This is a unique partnership anywhere in the world, and a most worthwhile achievement in Africa in itself.

- *Second*, the creation of a new field of scientific endeavour, namely **insect science** (in place of classical entomology), which brings together an array of scientific disciplines (physiology, biochemistry, biophysics, biomathematics, molecular sciences, genetics, ethology, social sciences, ecology, etc.) to understand the life and times of insect species in relation to their hosts and the environment, so as to design more rational means to manage their populations for the sustainable benefit of man. This new endeavour was created during the planning of a new international scientific journal concentrating on tropical insects, and has greatly been fostered by the ARPPIS educational programme.

- *Third*, introduction of a semester of required coursework to bring up the level of knowledge of modern insect science among the ARPPIS scholars for the Ph.D. degree, before they actually start on thesis project research.

- *Fourth*, the establishment of an Academic Board, in which all partner institutions are represented, and which decides policy issues regarding the academic programme, the exchange of staff, and the maintenance of a high level of excellence and relevance through regular monitoring and inspection.

- *Fifth*, the continuing close communication maintained by the ICIPE, as manager of the ARPPIS network on behalf of all partner institutions, of all ARPPIS graduates among themselves (through the founding of an ARPPIS Graduates

Alumni Association), and with the ARPPIS partner institutions (through periodic R & D conferences, the first of which was convened in December 1990), and the initiation of a Newsletter.

There is no doubt that the network conceptual and operational framework has out-yielded our best expectations. Any new developments, to enhance the content and quality of the ARPPIS network, must conserve and utilise these factors of success to the utmost.

Expansion of the ARPPIS Programme

The intensification of PESTNET activities within Africa over the last five years has demonstrated the sparseness and fragility of the human resource capacity in most African countries in insect science and its application to pest management. There is therefore tremendous demand, coming through PESTNET channels, for well-trained postgraduates in insect science to satisfy this long-term need. Similarly, the very success of the ARPPIS programme has accentuated the demand from universities for academic and research staff in insect science to man a large number of vacancies in the Participating Universities, as well as in those who are still outside this network. There is therefore no doubt that the ARPPIS network must grow and develop to contribute to the solution of this demand problem, which normally would be expected to be met solely from the postgraduate programmes of Universities, both African and foreign. This fact is recognised in the solutions advanced by the **Task Force Appointed to Make Recommendations on the Future Development of Graduate Training at the ICIPE**, which forwarded its Final Report in May 1989 (ICIPE Task Force, 1989).

The Task Force reinforced the effectiveness of the ARPPIS concept. It stated its overall assessment clearly and firmly:

> "The Task Force considered ARPPIS in depth and commended the unique structure of the network, combining, as it does, the strengths and ambitions of both an international research centre and of African universities. It considered it a model for the development of other educational degree networks in Africa for other disciplines."

In making definitive recommendations for the future, the Task Force put forward a two-pronged approach, to solve some of the operational difficulties that had arisen (such as lateness in the registration of scholars, long delays before Ph.D. examinations are completed), and to meet the enormous demand for qualified postgraduates, as well as meeting the large and diversified needs of PESTNET countries, the Participating Universities, the regional R & D centres, and the private sector.

The Task Force recommended that four **Sub-Regional Centres for the M.Sc. Degree in Insect Science** be mounted within the ARPPIS framework, each sub-serving a different sub-region in Africa, and in this way trying to meet the critical demands for postgraduates in that area. Each Sub-Centre will have as its focal point and programme manager one of the ARPPIS Participating Universities in the Sub-Region. Three have already been selected: University of Zimbabwe in Harare, to subserve the whole of Southern Africa; University of Ghana at Legon, to subserve English-speaking West Africa; and Dschang University Centre in Dschang, Cameroon, to subserve the entire French-speaking Africa. A mission to select the focal point for the East and North-Eastern sub-region has already done some work, and it should complete its deliberations in the next few weeks. When these Sub-Regional Centres become operational from mid-1992 to mid-1994, they will be admitting some 80 scholars each year for the two-year M.Sc. programme, comprising both coursework and a dissertation project. Apart from bringing out about 70 M.Sc. graduates a year, these programme management centres will progressively become centres of considerable research in insect science.

Contribution of an ICIPE Graduate School

These four Sub-Regional Centres and the proposed **ICIPE Graduate School in Insect Science** will, together, make the ARPPIS network a veritable mechanism for excellence in insect science postgraduate education and research. The Ph.D programme of the Graduate School will be the same programme in terms of its thesis research. It will continue to admit only a limited number of scholars as before, between 15 and 20 a year, for a programme which takes roughly three years. Otherwise, the programme will be different in three vital areas" (ICIPE, 1991b).

1. Although the Graduate School will not be a university, it will act as one in terms of its academic autonomy, having its own Academic Council (and a Dean as its chief executive) to undertake academic policy decisions, to monitor the performance of the Graduate School, to make rules and regulations for administering this institution, and to make appointments to the Faculty.

2. The Graduate School will have the power, under the relevant Kenyan laws, to award its own degrees — once it is accredited under Kenya's universities accreditation rules (Establishment of Universities Standardization, Accreditation and Supervision Rules, published under Legal Notice No. 56 dated 3rd March 1989[1].

The ARPPIS programme had not graduated any students before 1st August 1985, when the Universities Act (Cap. 210B) came into functional being. Consequently, ARPPIS and its associated ICIPE Graduate School can apply to the Commission for Higher Education as a "new university" under the Act. Under these circumstances, the Graduate School will be able to admit students who can take one of two options: register for the ICIPE Graduate School degree; or register for the degree of an ARPPIS Participating University as before.

3. The ICIPE Graduate School will considerably boost its opportunities for selecting first-class and experienced professors for short- or long-term appointments under the **Professorial Fellowship Scheme**. Such professorial fellowship appointees will not only devote significant time in teaching in their own specialist areas not well covered by ICIPE's own regular staff, but will also be enabled to devote some time to research as well.

---

[1] Under these Rules, "accreditation" means "public acceptance and confirmation evidenced by grant of charter under section 12 of the [Universities] Act that a university meets and continues to meet the standards of academic excellence set by the Commission [for Higher Education]...In this context, and for this purpose only, the ICIPE Graduate School would be regarded as a university. In the sense of the Rules, a "University" means "any institution or centre of learning by whatever name called, or however designated, having as one of its objects the provision of post-secondary education which intends to offer or is in fact offering courses of instruction leading to the grant of certificates, diplomas and degrees, and the expression 'university education' shall be construed accordingly." The description includes any agent or agency of such university within Kenya. In this respect, therefore, ARPPIS falls under the purview of these Rules - whether or not the issue of the ICIPE Graduate School is being considered, as Rule 3(2) is quite specific: "...[No] university shall - (a) advertise or continue to advertise or in any manner hold itself out to the public as a university; or (b) admit or continue to admit students to or conduct courses or programmes of instruction leading to the award of certificates, diplomas or degrees; or (c)otherwise embark upon or continue with any activity preparatory to the establishment of facilities for university education, after the commencement of these Rules without the authority of the Commission or of any other person competent to grant such authority under the Act".

The Future Prospects

The further development of ARPPIS to encompass four Sub-Regional Centres for the M.Sc. Degree in Insect Science, and the restructuring of the existing Ph.D. Programme in Insect Science at the ICIPE into an ICIPE Graduate School, will likely have an exhilarating effect on Africa's capacity to create, absorb, and use new knowledge in insect science and pest management. It is acknowledged that world-class university-based programmes of R & D in insect science, and of first-class postgraduate education in this discipline, could well turn out to be the breeding grounds for the mastery of insect science and its technological applications. In this scenario, the ICIPE has a vital part to play as a partner in high-level modern training and also as an advanced centre for R & D in tropical insect science.

We, the members of the ARPPIS network, very much hope that the donor community will steadfastly support this continuing successful experiment in postgraduate education in an important area of great social and economic impact in the tropics. We also hope the academic and research communities will encourage the implementation of an innovative programme to invigorate the human resource development scene in Africa, which has encountered such a seemingly endemic crisis in recent years. It could probably take a practical step in this direction if four or five major donors interested in higher education and R & D in Africa were to form a consortium to fund this newly upgraded and invigorated ARPPIS network, with four centres for postgraduate education and the ICIPE Graduate School. This can be viewed as a pilot project, which could be emulated for other areas of S & T if it succeeds in this specialised field of insect science. The operational budget required will probably be in the region of U.S. $400,000 a year for each Sub-Regional Centre and about U.S. $830,000 a year for the ICIPE Graduate School.

The ICIPE Graduate School, if recommended by Bellagio II and if later endorsed by the Governing Council of the ICIPE, could be accredited by Kenya's Commission for Higher Education through its vigorous system of inspection and visitation within a year. Consequently, it could become functional by March 1993.

References

Fenton, J.M. 1990. Soedjatmoko remembered: "Learn to learn to leave room for the unexpected." *UNU Work in Progress* **13** (1): 12.

ICIPE Task Force 1989. *Final Report of the Task Force on Recommendations of the Future Development of Graduate Training at the ICIPE.* The International Centre of Insect Physiology and Ecology (ICIPE), Nairobi.

ICIPE 1991a. *Strategic Framework for the 1990s.* Draft, March 1991. ICIPE, Nairobi.

ICIPE 1991b. *Graduate Training in Insect Science at the ICIPE: Planning Document.* Revised Draft Mimeo, May 1991. ICIPE, Nairobi.

Rabinowitch, V. 1986. *Lessons from History.* ICIPE Science Press, Nairobi.

LIST OF PARTICIPANTS

Dr. Olusola A. Adeyeye
Biology Department
Duquesne University
PITTSBURGH, PA 15282
United States of America

Fax: (412) 434-5780
Tel: (412) 434-5657 or 6332

Dr. A. Badran
Assistant Director General for Science
United Nations Educational, Scientific and Cultural Organisation (UNESCO)
7 Place de Fontenoy
75700 PARIS 1
Rue Moillis 75015
France

Fax: (33) 1 43-061-122
Tel: (33) 1 45-681-000
Tlx: 270-602

Dr. Oebele Bruinsma
Netherlands Organisation for International Cooperation in Higher Education
NUFFIC Africa Desk
Dadhuisweg 251
Box 90735
2509 LS
THE HAGUE
Netherlands

Fax: (31) 70-351-0552
Tel: (31) 70-351-0680

Prof. Zbigniew T. Dabrowski
Head of Institutional Building and Interactive Research Unit
The International Centre of Insect Physiology and Ecology (ICIPE)
P.O. Box 30772
NAIROBI
Kenya

Fax: (254) 02-803360
Tel: (254) 02-802501
Tlx: 22053 or 25066

Prof. J.S. Djangmah*
Zoology Department
University of Ghana
P.O. Box 82
LEGON
Ghana

Tlx: 2556

* Officially representing Prof. Donald E. Ekong, Secretary-General, Association of African Universities (AAU).

Prof. C. Ejike
Vice-Chancellor
Anambra State University of Technology
Independence Layout
PMB 01660
ENUGU
Nigeria

Tel: (042) 331244 or 331253
Tlx: 51405 or 51440

Prof. Mendathir El-Tingari
Vice-Chancellor
University of Khartoum
P.O. Box 321
KHARTOUM
Sudan
Tel: 72601-200
Tlx: 22113

Prof. Peter Esberg
Royal Veterinary and Agricultural University
Bulowsvej 13
Frederiksberg
DK-1870 COPENHAGEN
Denmark
Fax: 45-1-313-73193

Prof. George Eshiwani
The Principal
Jomo Kenyatta University College of Agriculture and Technology (JKUCAT)
P.O. Box 62000
NAIROBI
Kenya
Tel: (0151) 22646/9

Prof. James O.C. Ezeilo
Director
National Mathematical Centre
PMB 118
ABUJA
Nigeria
Fax: (09) 523-0783

Prof. Lameck K.H. Goma, MP, MCC
Minister of Higher Education, Science and Technology
P.O. Box 504640
15101 Ridgeway
LUSAKA
Zambia
Fax: (260) 1-252-951
Tel: 40406

Prof. Kunthala Jayaram
Director
Centre for Biotechnology
Anna University
GUINDY, Madras 600025
Tamil Nadu
India
Fax: (91) 44-235-299
or (91) 44-417-299
Tlx: 29096

Dr. M.T. Mapuranga
Assistant Secretary-General for Finance and Administration
Organisation of African Unity (OAU)
P.O. Box 3243
ADDIS ABABA
Ethiopia
Fax: (251) 1-513036
Tel: 514168

Prof. Maurice Ntahobari
Rector
National University of Rwanda
B.P. 56
BUTARE Fax: 30870
Rwanda Tlx: 22605

Prof. Thomas R. Odhiambo
Director
The International Centre of Insect Physiology and Ecology (ICIPE)
P.O. Box 30772 Fax: (254) 02-803360
NAIROBI Tel: (254) 02-802501
Kenya Tlx: 22053 or 25066

Mrs. Rhoda A. Odingo
Chief Planning Officer
The International Centre of Insect Physiology and Ecology (ICIPE)
P.O. Box 30772 Fax: (254) 02-803360
NAIROBI Tel: (254) 02-802501
Kenya Tlx: 22053 or 25066

Prof. Simeon Ominde
Professor of Geography
Institute of Population Studies
P.O. Box 30271
NAIROBI
Kenya Tel: (254) 02-332690

Prof. Dr. Heinz Rembold
Head, Insect Biochemistry
Max Planck Institute for Biochemistry
D-8033 Martinsried near Munich Fax:(089) 8578-3777
MUNICH Tel: (089) 85781
Federal Republic of Germany Tlx: 521740

Prof. Y.P. Singh
Professor of Agricultural Extension
Indian Agricultural Research Institute (IARI)
NEW DELHI 110012 Fax: (91) 575-2006
India Tlx: 3177161

Dr. Erik W. Thulstrup
Education and Employment Division
The World Bank
1818 H. Street, NW
WASHINGTON, DC 20433 Fax: (202) 477-0142
United States of America Tel: (202) 477-1234

Dr. Horacio H. Vanegas
The Director
Instituto Venezolano de Investigaciones Cientificas Venezuela (IVIC)
Apartado 21827
CARACAS 1020-A Fax: (582) 571-2557
Venezuela Tel: (582) 501-1122/23/24

GROUP PHOTO

Participants of the International Conference on Innovative Approaches for Sustainable Capacity Building for Insect Science Leadership in Africa, at the Rockefeller Foundation Bellagio Study and Conference Centre, Villa Serbelloni, Bellagio, Italy. June 24-28, 1991.